Homeschool Gone

Inspired Learning through Living

Homeschool Gone *Wild*

Inspired Learning through Living
Karla Marie Williams

ISBN 978-1983301742

Publisher: BeBold Publishing
Author: Karla Marie Williams
Language: English
Printed in the U.S.A.
First Edition

Table of Contents

Dedication

To my amazing and wonderfully supportive husband. Without you, I never would have attempted this project. Your support and encouraging push made it all possible.

To the Sensational Six. I never would have had the ability to experience this remarkable and life-giving journey without you. You are the ones that have shown me how to let go, how to be free, and how to approach life outside the box. For that, I am forever grateful.

"Karla Marie Williams' *Homeschool Gone Wild* is an inspiring read that will transform your ideas about education. It might also change your perception of unschooling! With enthusiasm and honesty, Karla shares her own homeschooling journey, answers common concerns, and offers lots of practical ideas and suggestions. If you haven't yet found your homeschooling happy place, this book is for you. Read it, and you might also end up homeschooling on the wild side!"

Sue Elvis
Stories of an Unschooling Family - Australia

Introduction

"The children are the curriculum."
— Lisa Murphy

Learning is a lifelong journey! It is not to be boxed or limited to specific days of the week, hours of the day, or times of the year. If we are breathing, we are learning. Our children's brains don't turn on at 8 a.m. and shut off at 3 p.m. Neither should their learning environment be limited by these standards of measurement.

This is a revelation that I had to come to after unsuccessfully homeschooling for almost four years. When I say unsuccessfully, I don't mean that my kids spent four years doing nothing. It was the fact that my desire for authentic and inspired learning had not taken place. It was forced, coerced, and dry. The moment I threw all caution to the wind and all of our textbooks out the window, the real journey began.

Our transition from a rigid and dry homeschool life to a wide open, inspired, and interest-led environment has been a complete game changer for our family. I have been considered crazy by traditional homeschoolers and not crazy enough by radical unschoolers.

Some call it unschooling. Others call it interest-led learning, life learning, life schooling, world schooling, or child-led learning. Whatever you call it, it can revolutionize your homeschool. Throughout this book, I will refer to unschooling and interest-led learning interchangeably.

I wrote this book for all the homeschoolers who may be dissatisfied with what they are doing and want to pursue something different. For all of those unschoolers who feel like they don't fit into anyone's learning style box, this is for you. Also, for the parents who may want to delve into their children's passions even if they are traditionally schooled, there is plenty of inspiration here for you too.

I did not write this book to convert homeschoolers to unschoolers. I pray that you will be inspired to continue to do what works for you and discontinue what does not. I pray our journey will motivate you to step outside the box and try new things.

This book will take you on a journey. Take a walk on the wild side with us and experience the freedom of inspired learning.

This is HOMESCHOOL GONE WILD!

Part One: Our Journey to Homeschooling

Chapter 1
In the Beginning

"Have patience. All things are difficult before they become easy."
— Saadi

One of the most life-changing years of our lives was 2006. After having several miscarriages over a period of years, we were finally parents. We adopted a three-year-old, a two-year-old, and a newborn who were siblings, all within a six-month period. It was parenting boot camp. We were in absolute Heaven. All of our dreams for a family had finally come true.

After quitting my job to stay home with the kids, I was determined to be THAT mom. You know, the one that can do it all. The mom that holds it all down at home, at work, at church, and in the community. She keeps a perfect house and cooks healthy, delightful meals every day. She never yells or makes mistakes. June Cleaver in the flesh. Her children are ideal due to her flawless parenting. THAT mom! The mom I soon realized did not exist on our planet.

I spent the majority of that year at home with my babies. I enjoyed it, although, I must admit that I missed the professional world like crazy. I longed for a conference call and a project I could wrap my hands around.

I was surrounded by career women. The itch to work and climb the corporate ladder would not go away. I eventually gave in to it and began applying for jobs. I found one that fit my "dream job" description at the time in human resources. I was singularly in charge of all of the human resource functions of seven plants for a military defense manufacturing company. Guess who was on top of the world?

I started to question myself. I was missing my children immensely. Having three small children under the age of three in daycare was taxing. It seemed like I was called at least two times a week to pick up someone due to an illness. Not to mention that the cost of daycare for three kids was overwhelming.

It became evident that I had to make a choice. Having it all at this season in my life did not seem to matter. I began to recall a quote that I had heard years before. "You can have it all. Just not at the same time or in the same season." I waited years to become a mom and I wanted to experience it to the fullest.

I was fighting a battle inside between the corporate world and motherhood. I knew that there would be hard days. There would be days when I would sit at dinner with my friends and have nothing to contribute to the conversation regarding a job, promotion, or significant accomplishment. I was okay with that. I was ready to take that plunge.

In January 2007, I chose to stay home with my children for the foreseeable future. I was settled and confident. As I settled into stay-at-home-mom life, I began to enjoy watching my children learn and grow firsthand. Our days were relaxed and full of wonder as they explored everything around them. This was the life.

I had heard of homeschooling in the past, but I had never given it much thought. That fall my oldest daughter was supposed to start school. I had a lot of questions.

"You can have it all. Just not at the same time or in the same season."

Should I send her to school? Should I try this homeschool thing? What if I mess her up? What if I don't have what it takes to do it well? We lived across the street from one of the highest ranked elementary schools in the city. What could go wrong with a reputation like that?

As August rolled around, I became unsettled in my own abilities. I was afraid I didn't have the patience. What were my friends and family going to say? Is this really legal? Can I homeschool her with two small kids underfoot? I pretty much talked myself out of it. A week after school started, I chickened out of homeschooling and enrolled her in school. It was the beginning of a battle that would break my heart.

Chapter 2
What Now?

"When a flower doesn't bloom, you fix the environment in which it grows, not the flower."
— Alexander den Heijer

Enrolling my daughter in school that fall was a huge mistake. I look back on it and wonder why I didn't trust myself. Why did I feel that I could not give her what she needed? Why didn't I realize that there is not a person on the face of this earth who is more vested in the outcome of her future than I am as her parent? Why?

We can ask ourselves all kinds of questions about the past. The reality is that we can only do something about tomorrow. What took place those next two years was not a pleasant experience for my daughter or for us as her parents.

"There is not a person on the face of this earth who is more vested in the outcome of her future than I am as her parent."

School #l
My child came home most days with a RED mark on her report. It was rare that she had a GREEN or even a YELLOW mark. They said she talked too much. She was disruptive. She did not follow instructions. She influenced others to mimic her "bad" behavior. She left the classroom without permission. The list goes on and on. My child was labeled as one of the school's "problem kids." They wanted to put her on medication, and they suggested counseling and stronger discipline at home. I was fed up. As her mom, I knew that my child was doing more right than she was doing wrong.

School #2
This was a Montessori school. Surely with a looser structure, she would thrive. Not so much. She was leaps and bounds above those in her class, and her boredom became a breeding ground for misbehavior. We began to see the same pattern taking shape.

School #3
The third time is always a charm, right? She had an excellent teacher. He really tried his best to connect with her and meet her needs – to no avail. Her disruptions were so intense that he had to have someone come work with her alone while he taught the rest of the class. During math lessons, she would cry, and he could not get her to do her work. All of the work that she was assigned to complete in class ended up coming home with her. I found myself teaching concepts and overseeing her schoolwork.

Eventually, they assigned her a school counselor to spend time with each week. It became painfully apparent that my child was, yet again, becoming THAT kid.

That Kid
You know the one. The one all the teachers joke about in the lounge. The kid who spends more time in the principal's office than they do in an actual classroom.

THAT kid. The one who your kid tells you about at the end of the day and you warn them to find other friends. The child many write off as a failure before they even get started.

There are precious children in our school systems across the nation - kids who need something different. The ones who need someone to care enough to investigate why a child is behaving the way they are before labeling them.

That was my child! I was committed to her, and I was no longer willing to let others label or speak ill of her. I needed to take her learning into my own hands.

Something had to be done. But what? In a moment of desperation, I contacted the only person I knew who homeschooled and asked her a million questions. Was I ready for this? Was this the right thing to do? Were we running from her challenges instead of facing them? Were her challenges magnified by the school system? Would I be able to do better than they did? Would I be in over my head?

Chapter 3
The Journey Begins

"What is most important and valuable about the home as a base for children's growth into the world is not that it is better than the schools, but that it isn't a school at all."

— John Holt

We did it! By Spring Break of 2009, we were at our wit's end. We had to help our child in any way we could. We could not let her fall between the cracks or let her self-esteem be destroyed based on the perception of others. It was "sink or swim" time. We chose to homeschool. Her academics were the least of our concern. She was a smart cookie. Our primary concern was that she needed more of us. More of a parental connection that she missed in her very early years before we adopted her. It became apparent that her struggles in school were the result of both early trauma and the need for a drastically different learning environment.

My husband and I were known for dancing to the beat of our own drum among our friends and family. However, our choice to homeschool was not a celebrated one. They thought we were careless, overprotective, and religious. We had gone rogue. Just like other decisions in our lives, we plowed forward without their approval and decided to do it anyway. The lack of support and loneliness was overwhelming at times.

At the time, I still had the baby at home, who was three years old. I also had my second oldest child in a kindergarten program, and he was doing well. That was, until he asked if there was something wrong with him. He thought everyone else got to stay home and learn because I loved them more. That broke my heart. It was at this point that homeschooling changed from a mission to save my daughter into a family affair.

I knew nothing about homeschooling and only knew one person who did it. I ordered everything she used. It was a massive box with five subjects that was supposed to last an entire school year. My very organized brain appreciated the easy open-and-go method as a beginner.

My husband came home one day and mentioned a co-worker of his who was a homeschool dad. His wife offered to spend some time with me. I took her up on her offer. She had four children and had already graduated three of them. As an ER doctor, she had no idea how she would pull it off. This mom decided to work nights in the ER and homeschool her children during the day. Her encouragement was crucial at that stage for me. She showed me all the programs she used and her mega-organized system and schedule that made me look like an absolute slacker. When I left her home that day, my mind was all over the place. The fact that an ER doctor could pull off homeschooling four children into graduation was astounding to me. I also considered my own insecurities, feeling like I did not measure up to her standard of organization and her rigid scheduling.

Again, I found myself doubting my ability to really do this and do it well. Was this the standard? Was the curriculum I had all there was? What was I missing?

I worked tirelessly to turn an empty room in our basement into a classroom. Posters, chalkboards, desks, matching book boxes and supply cases, file cabinets, and everything else that resembled an elementary class. My kids were excited. We were going to do this. I was so proud of my classroom that I showed it off to anyone remotely interested.

Why I thought my three-year-old would sit still while I "taught" is beyond me. I would stand in front of the kids' desks and literally try to teach things. He was under the table, kicking and playing with toys. The six-year-old was over it faster than I could get my teacher's manual open. The only one who was remotely compliant was my seven-year-old. She was familiar with this method; it was school at home. It was mayhem.

My husband came home many days to a teary-eyed and fed-up mom. I was questioning myself and all that I envisioned. This was horrific, stressful, and boring. We were not enjoying it one bit. I thought this was supposed to be liberating and fun.

After several breakdowns, my husband did what most husbands are programmed to do: solve problems. His solution was to send them back to school. Every time he would suggest this for my sanity, I would get a pit in my stomach. I had to pull it together. There was no way we were sending them back.

It was not long before we abandoned our windowless basement with all its bells and whistles in favor of our upstairs dining room. I stopped trying to "teach" in front of the classroom, and we just worked through our workbooks day after day. Five subjects, every single day: Bible, Math, Language Arts, History, and Science.

Changing the location in the home gave me the opportunity to otherwise entertain my three-year-old who moved like the speed of lightning. Things began to at least resemble progress or what I thought school was supposed to accomplish.

I assumed all would change academically for my seven-year-old at home, where the pressure was off and the overstimulated environment no longer existed. I was wrong. The excitement wore off pretty quickly and her days ended in tears after I pushed and forced hours of math and writing daily. My six-year-old was breezing through his workbooks at lightning speed but could not retain any of it a day later. The three-year-old was enjoying his pre-school activities and freedom from the basement dungeon. However, he would completely shut me down when I tried to teach him anything.

Learning is not supposed to be enjoyable, right? It was never fun for me, so I did not expect my children to do it without a fight. The unhappiness I saw in my kids did not register as a red flag. Instead, it was what I thought learning looked like due to my own experiences. What was I missing?

We plowed through this one-size-fits-all curriculum for the next three years. We plowed through life changes, job losses, and a temporary relocation from Michigan to Florida, and back to Michigan six months later. With each move and life change, homeschooling just became a part of the fabric of our family. In Florida, we took advantage of the weather and found ourselves "schooling" by the pool or in the park. Still, something was missing from our world of workbooks. It was dull, boring, and lacked depth.

"A shift in focus can ultimately change your relationship with your children."
— Rachel Racheous, *30 Days to Connected Parenting*

After moving back to Michigan, we continued with our workbook madness. They read stories, answered questions, and I checked their work. Lather. Rinse. Repeat. We added a homeschool co-op to our week. It did not last long after realizing that the same classes were offered every term without variation or creativity. I lacked the inspiration to do anything different, and the co-op was just as dry. What was I missing?

"They read stories, answered questions, and I checked their work. Lather. Rinse. Repeat."

Eventually, I began to join homeschooling pages on social media. Perusing these pages gave me lots of insight. I started to see families stepping outside of workbooks and into life. They were going on field trips and doing all kinds of hands-on experiments and activities. It was an entirely different picture of homeschooling than I had ever seen. I was inspired to do something different. But what?

The fear of messing up my kids kept me from venturing too far outside our boxed curriculum. I was afraid of ruining them. Afraid of doing something wrong. Worried that I would not have proof of what they did unless I had a completed workbook in my hands. I was stuck. I saw the light, but I was afraid to embrace it. Like many homeschool moms, I felt that I needed someone else's program or system. I needed someone to tell me what they needed to know next and what they should be doing at every age and grade. I didn't trust myself to let that go.

Even though I observed families online, none of them seemed to fit what I wanted for my kids. I envisioned something that I could not put into words. I could not describe it. It was something different.

Hearing the worry in other moms' voices when they discussed falling short of a scope and sequence created by someone else made me squirm. Was I supposed to be worried about that too? Why aren't I? Am I a slacker?

Hearing moms express fear over college choices for their small children was unbelievable. Seeing their rigid hour-by-hour schedules made me nauseous. I was not feeling it.

More than anything, it was my relationship with my kids that suffered. I prioritized the "work" over the connection. In the end, they were not retaining much. It was busywork, and in the process, a wedge was slowly pushing us apart.

Chapter 4
Sudden Changes

"There is no neutral education. Education is either for domestication or for freedom."

— Joao Coutinho

In 2013, our life changed drastically. After being a family of five for almost seven years, we decided to adopt three more children. This decision came with a lot of logistical issues. How on earth was I going to homeschool six children when I was already struggling with three? I needed a plan. Better yet, I needed a drastic change from what I was doing. It wasn't working, and I knew that it would not work with six.

I began reading blogs, books, and every single bit of information I could find on homeschooling styles. I kept running into information that told me that I had to be rigid and traditional. I had to do things a certain way for this to work. I was not buying it. I could feel what I wanted to happen, but I didn't have a picture of it. I was not sure if what I was envisioning had been done before.

Then I happened upon an unschooling blog. Although a lot of the information was very appealing to me, I have to admit that I was scared out of my mind. I thought they had to be nuts. Drop absolutely all curriculum and plans and merely live? How will their children learn that way? Education is supposed to be done in a particular manner. Aren't kids supposed to learn through textbooks that someone else has written? Don't they have to be taught?

This idea of unschooling or interest-led learning both excited and terrified me. I knew some elements of unschooling would not work for us, such as having a family of eight without assigned household help. Another aspect that was interesting to me about radical unschoolers was the fact that they seem to have very few rules for their household. Being the Type A personality that I am, I found it hard to see how that would work in our home. However, at this point, I was willing to try anything. I continued to ponder, pray, and research as much as I could on the topic.

When we brought our newest children home, we decided that our priority was building relationships and bonding as a family. I had all the time in the world to teach phonics, writing, and math, but I only had so much time to create a bond with them. So we decided to lay aside all formal lessons until further notice.

We decided that we would take off the entire summer and into the fall. We sat back and watched. I had read all about families who were succeeding with interest-led learning. They found freedom and joy in simply learning through life. Based on the boredom and the difficulties we had experienced homeschooling, I looked forward to experiencing this change. As I began to watch my children simply live, I noticed something exciting.

I saw how they started to learn on their own. I thought unschoolers were crazy until I began to see it work right before my eyes! It was actually real!

I read a lot of books and information on John Holt. He is the gentleman who coined the term unschooling. His knowledge was so intriguing to me. The way that he explained learning through life was refreshing. He wrote a book called *How Children Learn* that blew me away.

By doing and experiencing the real world, children experience real, meaningful, and inspired learning. That is what I wanted for my family.

Inspired learning is exactly what I began to see. Our children were teaching themselves things that we would never have initiated. They were also teaching each other new skills. It was a beautiful sight to behold.

"I thought unschoolers were crazy until I began to see it work right before my eyes!"

At the time, my husband was working outside the home more. He was not able to witness the excitement that I was experiencing. I would tell him about it, but he didn't really get it. He seemed to think that I was going a little off. He thought I had begun following something that wasn't going to be fruitful for our children. Being the optimistic man he is, he tried to be both supportive and objective.

It was not easy. When we were homeschooling traditionally, my husband never questioned what our days were like. He could see the workbooks and resources all over the house. It was evidence of their learning. When I went off the beaten path, he began to question everything. The pressure to test this idea and keep the peace with my husband was a lot to bear. Naturally, he was conditioned to see education one way. He has two degrees and he is a Marine. These things shaped his idea of systematic and formulaic instruction.

It is so important that parents are on the same page when it comes to making a change like this. This is not a homeschooling style. It is a lifestyle, and it affects everything in your home, your relationships, and the environment. If you have a spouse who is on the fence or dead set against what you are trying to do, you have to find a compromise. How can you meet the expectations of both of you? How can you show your spouse what you have observed and learned?

Later that year my husband's schedule changed, and he was home more often. That is when he had his light bulb moment. He began to see learning happen all around him without initiating it. He saw our children delve into topics and learn all kinds of things. Dad noticed how much they were getting out of self-inspired pursuits. He began to see how every single topic connected with them.

"Not only had we gone rogue when we decided to homeschool, but we were going further into the abyss in deciding to unschool."

Eventually, we were both sold. We saw children who had previously kicked against any type of formal lessons start to love learning. They were inspired by the world around them. This is what led to our final decision to embrace interest-led learning.

Not only had we gone rogue when we decided to homeschool, but we were going further into the abyss in deciding to unschool. This was not a popular choice. Those who had already questioned our decision to homeschool were really concerned at this point.

Thankfully, we were confident in the evidence that was surrounding us to embrace this lifestyle. We were living life and learning from the world around us as we followed the interests, passions, and God-given gifts of our children. We embraced this new freedom of inspired learning.

YouTube Companion Video

Channel: Karla and the Sensational Six

Videos:
Homeschool Authenticity
Homeschool Dads Rock
Why Interest-Led Learning?

Chapter 5
Unexpected Parenting Twist

"Sadly, in many cases, the assumption that children are incompetent, irresponsible, and in need of consistent direction and supervision becomes a self-fulfilling prophecy. The children themselves become convinced of their incompetence and irresponsibility and may act accordingly. The surest way to foster any trait in a person is to treat that person as if he or she already has it." — Peter Gray

We were convinced that we could not make radical unschooling work in our home. There was no way we were going to let this thing take over our entire lifestyle. We were willing to try the learning aspect, but all that other stuff was just too much. We could not give up all of our control. Boy, were we in for a surprise.

I never realized how much of a yeller and worrywart I was before pursuing this change. I had to come to the realization that my anger issues stemmed from not being able to control everything. I am far from where I want to be, but I am not where I was.

There was a lot of internal work that had to be done in us. It took time to recognize the things we were doing as parents that were counterproductive to our overall goals. It was essential for us to look at radical unschooling principles a little deeper before writing it off.

One of the things that I love so much about unschooling is that it changes everything around you. It is almost impossible to embrace this as a learning environment without embracing the other elements that change your life.

What I'm referring to is parenting. Unschooling drastically changed the way that we parent our children. We both have very strong personalities. As a result of that, we believe it really put a strain on our relationship with our kids. As we began to fall into unschooling, it helped us embrace who they were as individuals. Who God created them to be is magnificent, and we wanted to see them flourish as themselves.

One of my favorite parenting books is *The Five Love Languages of Children* by Gary Chapman. This book opened my eyes years ago to the individuality of my children and the fact that one-size-fits-all parenting just does not work. I noticed that the knowledge found in this fantastic book was a great complement to this new lifestyle.

Admittedly, we made some mistakes early in our parenting journey. We did not take into account the trauma that our children had suffered or their individual emotional needs due to their experiences before and while being in foster care. We came to the realization that we needed to change the way that we responded to our kids. We wanted to improve our relationship with them and contribute positively to their emotional health.

A part of radical unschooling that used to throw me off was now becoming quite apparent. I now understand how a family can abandon chores in favor of mutual respect for their living environment and each other. I used to be a complete drill sergeant when it came to tasks. We still have a list on the wall that serves as a reminder of our commitment to help around the house, but it is not a rope around our necks the way it was before. We are learning to be present and respond instead of reacting to them daily. When you are accustomed to doing things one way, changing is not easy, but it is necessary.

Our change began by starting with the heart of the matter, not the actual household duties. I would be untruthful with you if I told you that I am a 100% fuss-free momma. However, I am much more conscious of how I approach things today. We regularly discuss teamwork, accountability, mutual respect, and the value of a clean environment.

It does not mean that every day is smooth or that my children help out around the house with a huge smile on their face. No one wants to scrub the toilet. However, when we approach it from the heart of the matter, it helps us all do the hard things even when we would prefer not to. It helps when they see that we, as parents, are not asking anything of them that we are not willing to do ourselves. They learn by watching. We have begun to see them value their environment and volunteer to help more because of the heart change.

"We cannot expect them to learn to regulate their own bodies, appetites, emotions, schedules, and projects if we don't give them a chance to do it now."

I finally get how not having a bedtime helps a child regulate their own body and understand their individual needs. I used to be so focused on ending the day and putting the kids to bed that I never realized how it made them feel. One day my son said, "You like us more asleep than awake." He was joking, but you cannot imagine what that did to my heart. Of course, I never said that to them, but my enthusiasm for their bedtime had become offensive to the children that I love so much.

Don't get me wrong, I understand the value of time alone and personal time with my husband. I also realize that independence and self-regulation do not happen if we don't give our children the chance to do it. We cannot expect them to learn to regulate their own bodies, appetites, emotions, schedules, and projects if we don't give them a chance to do it now.

We started with our teens and worked our way down to the younger kids. We decided that they would no longer have a bedtime. I had no idea what the outcome of this decision would be. To this day, most of our kids have fallen asleep no later than eleven o'clock. When they go to sleep at night, it is because their bodies are tired, not because they were forced to. Giving them the freedom to listen to their bodies makes them aware of their own needs and helps them develop self-regulation skills.

I am always asking myself how I can give my kids more autonomy in learning, food, bedtimes, and a variety of choices that involve them.

I am a night owl. My kids are long gone by the time I retire for the night. I am still able to have quiet time and time to work uninterrupted. You can always adjust this to your own family's schedule.

This has become a complete lifestyle for us and more than a homeschooling style. Allowing our children more autonomy in their learning and other areas of their lives has brought back a spark and fire in their eyes.

YouTube Companion Video

Channel: Karla and the Sensational Six

Video: How Unschooling Changed Our Parenting

Part Two: A New Way of Thinking

Chapter 6
Unschooling Rules

"The future belongs to the curious. The ones who are not afraid to try it, explore it, poke at it, question it and turn it inside out."

— Unknown

As I mentioned before, I have been considered crazy by traditional homeschoolers, and accused of being too loose and unstructured. On the flip side of things, I have been considered an unschooling imposter because we don't do everything that radical unschoolers say we must do. I am comfortable with the fact that we don't fit into a preconceived box. Unschooling is the closest thing that describes what we do, and what we do works wonders for us.

We all want to know the steps to success for whatever we are pursuing. How do we do this? What is the magic pill? Is there a secret formula?

You have taken all the social media "what kind of homeschooler are you?" quizzes. You have dissected every single homeschool style and method to find yourself in them. You can tell me all the dos and don'ts of the Charlotte Mason style. Classical Conversations or Thomas Jefferson Homeschooling may have piqued your interest. You may have even purchased oodles of Montessori products because you believe in the ideas.

They all have clearly defined methods and philosophies.

So what are the rules of unschooling? What do you need to purchase? Where can you get a checklist? How does this thing work?

The "how" of unschooling or interest-led learning can be elusive. I am here to tell you that there are very few "rules."

I am going to let you in on a little secret. There are only three rules to unschooling. Yes. You heard that right.

There may be lots of theories and people who share what they do and how they do it. However, unschooling and all of the descriptions and "how to" instructions are narrowed down to these three things.

- Respect your child as an individual.
- Follow their lead in learning and interest.
- Nurture those interests.

That's it. Those are the rules.

Chapter 7
Misconceptions about Unschooling

"The illiterate of the 21st century will not be those who cannot read and write, but those who cannot learn, unlearn and relearn."
— Alvin Toffler

We have been taught to believe that learning can only take place in a classroom, at a desk, with thirty students the same age. We have been conditioned to think that everyone must learn the same thing, in the same way, at the same pace and age as everyone else. It is this belief that paralyzes us even when we see the benefit in doing something different. Here are some of the greatest misconceptions about unschooling or interest-led learning.

Faith and Unschooling
I have been asked, "How does unschooling fit within your faith?" Many believe that strict instruction and direction is the only way to raise a child that embraces your faith. They don't think unschooling lines up with the way scripture tells us to raise our children. I beg to differ. It fits perfectly within God's desires. Our goal as parents is to give our children the freedom to be who God called them to be.

The only things we do not encourage are interests that do not line up with our faith and values. We don't spend hours dissecting devotionals and hammering scripture into their heads. What we do is use everyday life to expose our children to God's words and ways. Our children embrace life, learning, and our faith by seeing our example, not by force.

Not for minorities

I have been told that minorities don't have the luxury of unschooling because we already have to work harder to achieve the same level of success as our counterparts. They feel that a traditional learning structure or system gives them a better fighting chance in an uneven world.

I do not agree with this. We raise our children to focus more on their faith and the person God called them to be than the color of their skin. Every privilege of accomplishing their destiny is possible in Christ; therefore, unschooling is as much for them as anyone else. I am not naive enough to think that they will not face the ignorance of others during seasons of their lives, but our confidence in Christ and God's design for their life transcends those fears and circumstances.

Unparenting

Unschooling does not mean unparenting. I cannot speak for every unschooling parent and family. Households are as different as the families that inhabit them. It is a prevailing thought that you don't parent or instruct your children at all if you are unschoolers.

The truth is, as an unschooling parent, you guide, nurture, and instruct your children respectfully versus a dictatorship. With wisdom and guidance, a parent makes the best decisions for their child, considering their desires, but ultimately doing what is best.

Laziness
There is this notion that unschooling families are lazy. I am more hands-on and involved in my children's lives now than I have ever been. Unschooling has required more of me than traditional homeschooling ever did in the past. Personally, I am a better parent today because I have tuned into who my children are as individuals and it has deepened the connection with each one of them. Unschooling is an active sport. We are always moving.

Children rule the home
Unschooling does not mean that you do not guide and nurture their souls. It does not mean that you do not invest in them and teach them life skills or principles. It means there is freedom for them to make some of the choices that affect them.

Again, we are not radical unschoolers, so we tend to have a few more "standard procedures" or "expectations" than some. However, we are much better than we used to be.

My children do not rule the household. They are, however, respected for their humanity, feelings, gifts, talents, and desires.

For younger children
A lot of people think that unschooling is cute and useful for small children but not for older children or teens.

They feel the older they get, the more stringent we need to be. In my experience, unschooling is just as rewarding for teens as it is for younger children. As a matter of fact, the older a child gets, they benefit from it even more, especially if they know what direction they want to go in the future.

They have a head start in that direction and the ability to get their feet wet long before their peers seeking the same careers and dreams.

Not for college-bound kids

An opinion held by many is that unschooling only works for kids that are NOT college-bound. They feel that you cannot possibly prepare a child for the rigor of college if you do not follow a rigorous and traditional path.

This could not be further from the truth. As a matter of fact, many unschooled teens are already taking college courses before their typical college years. The independence and self-inspired skills they gain are just what colleges and employers are seeking. I would guesstimate that the percentage of unschoolers that attend college is equivalent to the rate of traditional schoolers or homeschoolers that attend. Just like any other population, some do, and some don't. Later in this book, you will learn more about our oldest two kids, one who is a college-bound unschooler and one who is considering multiple paths. I will share how we prepare them for their particular road ahead. We do not believe that college is the only way for our children to succeed and accomplish their dreams.

Real world-readiness

"If kids get to choose what they do, when they do it, and how they do it, they will have a wake-up call in the real world." This is a prevalent opinion.

Unschoolers learn how to manage their time, resources, and behavior patterns in the "real world" every single day. Just like anyone else, having the freedom to choose gives them first-hand experience in what to do and not to do in many of life's situations. With guidance from their parents and room to make choices in the real world, they will be just fine.

Competitive edge

"I want my kids to have a competitive edge and shine above their peers." Many parents go for a one-size-fits-all education because they feel it levels the playing field for their child.

How much more competitive can a child be than to have exercised hands-on experience in the areas of their passion years before their peers. The goal should not be to outshine everyone but to be their very best. My child needs to be able to compete in the areas in which they are pursuing. If my child wants to be a dancer or a singer, why would I put the premium focus on all the things that will not encourage and strengthen those gifts? Likewise, if they want to be a doctor and I focus on performing arts, I am not doing them any favors. A competitive edge is entirely relative to the child and their interests.

Children will waste away

"If you allow your children to control their day, all they would do is play video games and watch television." This is one of the number one fears I hear from moms.

I don't think we give children enough credit for their intelligence and passions. I also don't think we give technology enough credit for being a tool in our modern world when used effectively.

If you create an atmosphere that includes other activities and things to do that are just as alluring, the video games would not be the only thing a child chooses. Later in this book, we will discuss this in further detail and how to keep technology in proper perspective.

Irresponsible

The boldest and most offensive misconception that I have heard to date is that unschooling is irresponsible and neglectful parenting. Anyone who has ever witnessed what we do and how we do it could never label us as reckless or negligent. It is quite the opposite for the majority of unschoolers! I cannot speak for imposters who use the label to do absolutely nothing. This opinion only comes from people who have no frame of reference for what unschooling actually is or how it works.

"When you get down to it, unschooling is really just a fancy term for 'life' or 'growing up uninstitutionalized.'"

— Grace Llewellyn

Statistics

Before I state the below statistics, let me be very clear. I do not do this based on my need for proof of success. I do not base my children's progress on others' standards of measurement but on their own individual goals for themselves.

Psychology Today conducted a "Survey of Grown Unschoolers" (June 2014) led by Peter Gray, Ph.D. They shared these statistics that were gathered from 232 unschooling families between 2011 and 2013. A further survey was completed in 2014 by 75 adults who were unschooled. These are the results of that survey. The number of unschoolers has risen significantly in the last several years. Their statistics and status seem to get lost among the general homeschooled population, which is why the sample number is small.

Pursued a form of higher education (college, trade school, etc.)	83%
Have earned a degree	44%
Begin advanced college courses	Age 16
Financially self-sufficient	78%
Entrepreneurs	53%

Correlation between childhood interest and current career 77%

7 out of 10 believe that the greatest benefit was self-motivation and confidence.

1 out of 2 unschooled teens pursued creative and technological careers.

Two-thirds of the respondents will unschool their own children.

High school grades 9-12 are the highest demographic of unschooled kids.

Sharing these stats is not my way of proving anything except the fact that a child in an unschooling atmosphere has the abilities and the same opportunities available to them as any other child. What is more important than the statistics themselves is the fact that unschoolers are more likely to be engaged in a career path that they are passionate about, which is what unschooling is all about.

YouTube Companion Videos

Channel: Karla and the Sensational Six

Videos:

FAQs about Child Led Learning
Warning: You Should Not Pursue Interest-Led Learning

Chapter 8
Living and Learning

"You will not reap the fruit of individuality in your children if you clone their education."
— Marilyn Howshall

Starting this journey toward an interest-led learning environment for my kids was both exciting and scary. It is so hard to rid yourself of the thoughts that tell you how learning is supposed to take place. Still, I plowed through information and paid attention to those who had gotten results from their children learning in this way.

Finally, the thing I had envisioned for my family was taking shape. I had a name for it and examples of people who were doing it. My mindset regarding how learning actually works began to transform. There was joy in their eyes again. Knowledge became something to embrace and not avoid.

Before the age of five years old, we are full of wonder. The world is a vast, open place full of possibilities and endless things to explore and learn. We delve into interests and passions, sometimes holding on to them for months or even years. We ask every question that comes to mind of any adult who will answer. We touch, smell, taste, watch, and listen to everything around us to figure out what this world is all about.

At five years old, we are whisked away into a world of "school." We are told what to think, how to think, and why to think it. There is no time to explore. No time for extra questions or curiosity. We must know a collection of things and prove our intelligence by regurgitating it so that we can move forward to another group of facts each year.

Between the ages of five and eighteen, we are deposited into, drilled, and tested continually like a machine on an assembly line as if all of our destination and purpose were the same. The public school system is not the only crowd that falls into this trap. Scores of homeschoolers fall for the same thing.

Then at age eighteen, we are told, "Go find your way. You are a grown-up now." We are expected to remember how to be ourselves. We have lost the wonder, curiosity, and drive to do anything without being forced or told. This is why a vast majority of adults do not read after high school or college. Reading was a task and a requirement. It was never a choice or something we did for enjoyment. After thirteen years of forced fact recall, testing, and competing, we have lost the drive and will to follow what interests us. Unfortunately, some of us never regain that wonder.

"Our large schools are organized like a factory for the late 19th century: top-down, command control management, a system designed to stifle creativity and independent judgment."
— David T. Kearns, CEO, Xerox

In a factory, every car that is on that assembly line has the same purpose. It is to safely get human beings from one place to another on wheels. The system to create them and make sure they can do their job is regulated and systematic to ensure the end goal is reached. Our children are not cars. They do not have the same purpose or destiny; therefore, they should not have the same learning experience.

Unschooling allows for our children to continue that wondrous, curious, and inspired drive to explore without a thirteen-year gap in the middle. That freedom they had at four is the same freedom they have to learn what they want to learn at eleven, twenty-three, and sixty-two. It is setting them up for a lifelong love of learning that will span decades and bring great joy and fulfillment.

Compulsory Education

In 1852, Massachusetts became the first state in the US to make attendance and systematic instruction mandatory. Eventually, all 50 states followed this mandate. This was when we began to demand that every child learn the same thing, in the same way, at the same time. It is referred to as industrialized or factory-style education. It is during this time period that children are robbed of their individuality, God-given drive, and tenacity to do what they love. Other tasks have been placed higher on the list of importance.

The Industrial Age changed the way that we educate our children. During this period of time, our goals as a society were to man factories and build industry. We now live in a different age where soft skills, creativity, and innovation are the highest qualities on the list of employers and clients. If our world is different, then our approach to learning must also be different.

"Unschooling allows for our children to continue that wondrous, curious, and inspired drive to explore without a thirteen-year gap in the middle."

When you look at unschooling as merely a "type of homeschooling" or a "learning style," you miss the point. It is a lifestyle! It is living as if school does not exist. It is following the interests and passions that make you who you are, a way of thinking that permeates your entire life. Everyone in the home is involved in the seeking and becoming of who they were created to be, including the parents. It really is impossible to partially unschool. You either do, or you don't.

Chapter 9
Breaking the Mold

"Everybody is a genius. But if you judge a fish by its ability to climb a tree, it will live its whole life believing that it is stupid."
— Albert Einstein

If you have investigated homeschool styles, you may have heard words like rubric, scope, and sequence (standard measurements by grade), or the lists of "what your child should know in second grade." These may have been comforting to you or a thorn in your flesh. For me, they were the latter.

I would be up at night worried that my child could not do something that the list said they should be able to do. It bothered me that my child did not know what "everyone" else knew at their age.

In my observation, I had a child who detested writing but was a scientist at heart. I had another child who had a fear of numbers and math but was a talented writer. Still another child didn't embrace formal learning but could tell me more than I have ever known about world history, war, and natural disasters. An entirely different child was dealing with a speech impediment but was obsessive about medicine and surgeries. I used to focus on what they struggled with so much that I missed their brilliance and natural talents.

I mention these things as an example of maximizing your children's strengths. When we are adults, we recognize we have strengths and weaknesses. We have things that we are good at and things that we don't do well. Why do we assume that children are any different? Exercising our strengths and strongest passions are what make us happy and fulfilled. Acting as if everyone needs or should have the same body of knowledge or that they need to perfect the same things is absurd.

If we were honest with ourselves, we would realize that very few children master everything at the same time, certainly not at the same age and perceived grade level. Every person is different. I had to be alright with that.

We worry ourselves and put pressure on our children to learn within the framework and boundaries created by someone else - someone who does not know them or understand their gifts and abilities.

Undue pressure to go faster or slower than their natural pace creates an unmotivated learner. Every child needs to be able to determine how they learn and at what speed they learn.

We look at these lists and we think to ourselves that our children are behind. Behind whom? The learning and the track that they are on needs to be their own. Their goal needs to be a self-challenge of their own skills and talents.

People do not learn the same things, at the same time, in the same way, for the same reasons. A system like this will crush the dreams and spirits of a lot of children who feel they need to measure up to someone else's list instead of the one they create for themselves.

"Behind whom? The learning and the track that they are on needs to be their own."

I urge you to throw away the lists. I implore you to allow your child to learn and develop as they pursue their interests on a timeline set for them as an individual.

Chapter 10
Not So Smooth Transitions

"All I am saying can be summed up in two words: Trust Children. Nothing could be simpler, or more difficult. Difficult because to trust children we must first trust ourselves, and most of us were taught as children that we could not be trusted."

— John Holt

I would love to say that transitioning to interest-led learning from our previous way of doing things was a smooth transition. It wasn't. I was still riddled with doubt and questioned whether I had lost my mind. I was my own worst enemy. This kept putting temporary halts on our progress. All of my children reacted differently to this transition, and I had to figure out how to help them all through it.

My oldest daughter, who was ten at the time, was confused. She did not trust me. Even though she did not enjoy what we had been doing, she still felt weird about making such a drastic change. Today, she loves her freedom.

My oldest son was nine when we transitioned to unschooling. He had the hardest time out of all of my children. He was frustrated with the lack of instruction, and I was disappointed with his lack of initiative, which I interpreted as laziness. It took us a while to find a groove with him. What he needed was the freedom to choose what, when, and how he learned. However, the resources needed to be traditional. It was a huge light bulb moment. Today he is thriving! He tells me what he wants to learn and I find classes and books to help him do it.

My youngest four children were six, six, five, and three at the point of transition. They were still young and had never experienced a traditional school environment. Like most small children, they saw "school" on TV and in movies and looked forward to the day when they would experience that. Of course, I knew that their experience would not be like the one they saw on the screen. When we transitioned to unschooling and changed the environment in our home, they were a little disappointed. They were not disappointed that they were going to be able to pursue their interests, but they grieved that they would not experience "school" like they thought it would be.

Having their own desks, changing classes, lunchroom food fights, and school bus rides sounded exciting to them. Today, they flourish daily, and I am astounded by their initiative and desire to learn all they can learn about all the things that cross their path.

During this transition, I had to keep my head up and know that I was on the right track, because my kids were not so sure. I am an all or nothing personality. I am tunnel focused on things I want to accomplish. I had to decide and be confident in what I was doing and go at it with reckless abandon. That is precisely what I chose to do. I decided to not look back and I decided to trust what I was observing. This was a shift in perspective and thought for our entire family.

How do I transition?

You may be asking, "How in the world can I go from where I am to where I want to be?" The answer to that depends on a variety of things. It depends on your confidence in the outcome of this change and your willingness to let go. It can also depend on your support system and your spouse's comfort level with the transition.

There are two ways to go about transitioning to a more interest-led learning environment. One is cold turkey, like me, or slowly loosening the reigns.

Cold turkey

Sometimes you are convinced that drastic measures have to be taken to preserve your child's love of learning. You have had it and are ready to throw everything out the window.

This was me. I had done my research and studied it long enough to be confident that this was what my family needed. Even though we fell into it sooner than we had planned, we went for it. We took advantage of the pause in our life after adopting our youngest three children to transition and we never turned back.

When you go cold turkey, everyone has to be on the same page. You have to openly communicate with your spouse and children about what is happening and how things will change. You have to get their opinions and desires, as well as answer any questions that they may have about this new lifestyle. How does your spouse envision the change?

How do your children envision this change? Get feedback on their vision for their new learning environment.

You STOP what you are doing and make a hard right toward your goal. This is how we did it. I must admit that it took over a year for us to embrace other aspects of unschooling. That was thanks to my Type A personality and my husband's Marine background. We struggled with letting go of how we handled areas outside of learning.

Loosen the reigns

If your goal is just to loosen up a bit and allow your kids room to pursue their passions, then your transition will be less drastic. You or your spouse may want to hold on to some of the things you are doing. Every parent's goal is for their children to develop a love of learning.

The key is to keep doing what works and change what doesn't. When I say "what works," I don't mean that your children complete the work without complaining or much of a hassle. When I say "what works," I mean that the approach is enjoyable and leads to a love of learning.

Expand how you see education and how learning takes place inside and outside of a textbook. There are four ways that you can loosen up the learning environment in your homeschool.

- Decide together which areas you are willing to give up control in to allow your child to explore.
- How can you allow them to control their daily schedule?
- How can you let them choose how they go about learning a topic? Change the way information is presented to better suit their interests.
- What extracurricular activities will highlight their interests and passions?

"The key - keep doing what works and change what doesn't."

Fear is a thief

Periodic Unschoolers Panic (P.U.P.) is a real thing. You start experiencing the freedom you always wanted for your kids. You are seeing glimpses of hope and passion in your children's eyes after transitioning to interest-led learning. It feels so good!

Then it happens. The kids are quizzed at Thanksgiving by Uncle Bob, and they freeze up. Or maybe you happen to frequent a homeschool community page or co-op, and everyone is planning their next year and stressing over curriculum choices. You lose it! You start to panic. P.U.P. sets in and sends you into a complete tailspin. This has happened to the best and most confident of unschoolers.

We have fears that our children need certain bodies of knowledge to succeed in life. We have concerns that giving them the freedom to choose will not enable them to obtain those bodies of knowledge. I would venture to say that an engaging interest-led environment will include life skills and every other skill a child will need to achieve their life goals. Every topic taught in a traditional educational environment can be found and explored through living and applying it to life.

Micromanaging out of fear will rob you and your children of the learning experience you want so badly. It is rooted in fear of losing control. The fear of not having complete jurisdiction over every single detail and minute of our children's day stops us cold.

There are so many aspects of a child's day that can easily be handed over to them. If we trust them, they will surprise us time and time again with their ability to self-regulate in many areas. Take a moment and think about the areas of your child's life that you micromanage. Some of those areas are pointless and really don't require your oversight at all. Other areas are often our own insecurities or inability to release. They have nothing to do with our children's capacity to handle them.

My husband is very good at pointing this out to me. I no longer have small children that need me for a lot of things. One example of my micromanagement tendencies is my obsession with my kitchen and cleanliness. My husband asked me why I felt the need to make all the kids' meals when they are old enough to make their own breakfast and lunch. Then I would complain about it. I had to ask myself why. It was because I wanted the kitchen to remain clean. I also wanted to control how much of something they ate. Why? Why does any of that matter? It doesn't, but that was a control issue I had to get over. Today, as they do these things themselves they still make a mess, and yes they overindulge at times. The beauty of it is that my schedule is free and I can relax as they learn independence.

Talking about micromanaging our children goes far beyond what I mentioned above. It stretches into our homeschools. We become obsessed with controlling every single aspect of their education until we make learning a drag.

When you fluctuate back and forth between school-at- home and interest-led learning, you bring confusion and uncertainty into the situation. This is when your fear shows and your children don't know what you expect from them. This can cause them to not like homeschooling at all. It also causes your children to separate their interests, life, and play from learning. This should be the opposite of your goal.

I can remember doing this several times as we transitioned and it was a huge stumbling block to our progress. I would let go and then clam up and pull out the workbooks. My children's attitude towards learning or trusting me laid in the balance as I figured this thing out.

I have never met a child that would be disappointed with interest-led learning. NOT ONE! I have, however, met parents who were unwilling to let go long enough to watch it work. Just like anything else, it takes time.

Deschooling

Deschooling is a period of time set aside where you focus on relationships and living. Nothing remotely schooly or educational is introduced or expected during this time.

The general rule of thumb is to deschool one month for every year a child spent in a traditional school environment. However, this amount of time is entirely up to you.

We deschooled when our daughter was pulled from public school. We also deschooled when we transitioned from traditional school-at-home to unschooling. It takes time to adjust and reboot.

Deschooling gives you that time to solely focus on relationships and living while you both redefine what a natural and inspired learning environment will look like for you going forward.

YouTube Companion
Videos Channel: Karla and the Sensational Six
Videos: Micromanaging Our Children
How do I Transition to Interest-Led Learning? - Part 1
How do I Transition to Interest-Led Learning? - Part 2

Chapter 11
Free to Be

"A lot of parents will do anything for their kids except let them be themselves."
— Banksy

How many people do you know who spent thousands of dollars and countless years getting a degree that does not serve their interests? How many people work in an industry that they hate for decades because they think that their interests can only qualify as a hobby? Dare I estimate, many people you pass on a daily basis fit into this category. How many kids grow up fulfilling their parents' dreams instead of their own? Not on my watch!

I can say that now, but my actions in the past have shown otherwise. Dare I admit that, even after embracing unschooling, I made a lot of mistakes, mistakes based on pride, arrogance, and selfishness. Yes. This unschool momma has messed up several times, and I am here to tell you all about it. My prayer is that you don't make some of the same mistakes that I made.

My desire when I started this journey was to free my children from society's expectations and boundaries. I wanted them to be free to be themselves and accomplish God's plan for their lives. What I did not realize was that I still had expectations and boundaries I had built around them that they needed to be freed from.

The first encounter I had in confronting my own pride in this area happened in 2015. I was scheduled to speak at a conference in Zimbabwe. I was so excited to experience my third African country and make a difference in the lives of children.

A few months before I left, I decided to bring my oldest daughter along for this trip. She was 12 at the time. I desired to bond with and get closer to my daughter while showing her another part of the world. As we got closer to the trip, I shared as much as I could about the country, the orphan crisis, and what I would be doing while I was there. I wanted her to catch my vision and passion. I had crafted an idea in my heart of her taking up the same cross and following in my footsteps.

I celebrated my fortieth birthday in Zimbabwe that year. The conference went very well. We had the chance to see much of the country and all of its splendor, including a wildlife safari, animal sanctuary, magnificent terrain, and mountainous landscapes. This was amazing. What twelve-year-old gets to frolic about in the wilderness with wildebeests? She did. Then there were the not so easy things to experience, such as an unprecedented level of poverty and people who were hurting. She had an opportunity to see what I do when I travel all over the world. Surely, she would want to do this too, right?

We returned from our trip, and I expected a complete rebirth of my child. She would be an entirely different person. All kinds of revelations and epiphanies had to have come from such an enriching experience.

I instantly went into "school" mode. Since my daughter was not showing me outwardly how she was impacted by the trip, I decided to force it. I made her write me an essay about her thoughts. She did very well at detailing her experiences. I was still unsatisfied. I could not put my finger on it.

Being honest with myself, what I really wanted was for her to have the same passion that I have for the same things. I had to realize that at her age it was hard to articulate what she saw and experienced. It was the polar opposite of the life she lived every single day. My pride and selfishness wanted her to experience things through my eyes. The problem with that is she is a different person, and there is a twenty-seven year difference between our life experiences.

Is it possible that when she is thirty years old she will look back and see what an amazing experience she had been afforded? Possibly. I had to let her experience be her own. I could not make her feel what I felt, see what I saw, or even think what I thought.

I sat down one day, and I told her that I released her from the feeling that we had to be passionate about the same things. I apologized for putting the pressure on her to pursue something that was not her dream, but mine.

Ball Drop

Shortly after my conversation with her, I felt the need to have a round-table with all of my children. I needed them all to know that they were free to dream their own dreams and pursue their personal goals.

If you ever want to punch pride in the stomach, say you are sorry and admit your own mistakes to your children. Anyone who has been a parent for any amount of time knows that you will have plenty of opportunities to do this.

They all responded well to our conversation. The real test would come later when my children wanted to talk about their passions or change directions.

One such example was my oldest son. I must admit that I was proud to have a son who was flying planes at the age of thirteen. Who wouldn't be? This proves that interest-led learning works, right? One day he told me that this was just his first goal and he was not sure if this would end up being a hobby or a career. What? We spend all this money and effort to afford you these opportunities, and you don't know? He went on to explain that being a pilot was his first step in the aviation industry and that it would be his launching pad to other things.

I had to take a breath. I had to check my pride and forget about my bragging rights. This was my son's dream, not mine. Why was I so possessive? Why did I feel like I had the power to direct his goals for his future? I needed to step out of the way.

I had another opportunity to swallow my pride with my youngest daughter, who was dead set on becoming a doctor. She would spend hours immersed in medical videos, books, and activities. Her life's path was apparent, or so we thought. One day she came to her dad and mentioned a dream that she had. In that dream, she saw herself doing something completely different. She said that she was happy and fulfilled and thought that this was what she wanted to do. She wanted to go into performing arts.

You could say, "Great, what is wrong with that?" You know as well as I do that our society has conditioned us to believe that medical school leads to financial success. My momma-brain was thinking about her future security, financial stability, and happiness. I feared that my child would chase a Hollywood dream like thousands of others, disappointed and broke. My husband immediately switched gears with her. I did not. I am not proud to admit it. I was afraid.

I began to see her light up on stage when she started taking dance classes and pursuing other interests outside of medicine. I gained confidence that God had her future in His hands and that she would be alright. I had to remember that I did not create her or give her a purpose… He did.

My sweetheart is only eleven today, and she has her entire future ahead of her. She still enjoys the sciences, and she chooses to study them often. I am confident and at peace with whatever direction she follows and I give her the reigns to do so.

"They need to be able to change directions and dream their own dreams."

But Wait, There's More

One would think that I had learned my lesson from the mistakes I shared above. Unfortunately, my humanity sometimes gets in the way of my most genuine unschooling intentions.

One of my sons had mentioned for several months that he wanted to play the piano. After investigating the local opportunities, it seemed like it was not going to happen. We did not have a keyboard for him to practice on between lessons. Purchasing one anytime soon was not in the budget.

I had the brilliant idea of offering him his brother's old guitar. If a person loves music, they would like any instrument, right? I began to manufacture a goal for him to learn the guitar. He went along with it for a while, but there was no real enthusiasm. Here we were again. Mom was trying to give another child a dream that was not their own. He wanted to play the piano.

Once I got in line with the dream in his heart, I was able to direct all of my efforts toward making it happen for him. Shortly after that, a friend sent me a posting of a church moving sale. They had a piano for sale for pennies on the dollar. My son now has a piano of his own to pursue his interests and has completely fallen in love with music.

Why did I share all of this with you? I could pretend that I have always been the perfect unschooling mom. That would not be helpful to you at all.

If my children follow a path I have designed for them, then I have failed. If my children choose a college major or a job that I want them to choose, then I have failed. If my children can pass a standardized test with flying colors but cannot pursue the things that make them uniquely amazing, it is all for naught.

Sometimes we have to give ourselves grace for merely being human and making mistakes. We also have to learn to detach our pride from our children's accomplishments or dreams. Children need to have the ability to be honest with us. They need to be able to change directions and dream their own dreams. Pride, selfishness, and ulterior motives have no place in unschooling if we are going to give our children the freedom to be who God called them to be.

Chapter 12
Invitations to Explore

"Children are naturally creative. It is our job to give them the freedom, materials, and space to let their creativity blossom to its full potential."

— The Artful Parent

An inspiring environment promotes creativity and exploration. It invites curiosity and wonder. It engages the senses in multiple ways. A stimulating environment tickles all five senses.

We have lived in three homes since we started homeschooling back in 2009. In each home, we had a school room with all the bells and whistles. For some reason, I thought I needed this. I felt it validated our homeschooling status. Not one of those classrooms was utilized. We learn everywhere. Every single room in our house, yard, car, or anywhere we have gone became a place to learn. The world became our classroom.

By the time we embraced unschooling completely, we dismantled the classroom and the notion that this was a necessity for our new learning environment. Instead, we cleared that room and turned it into a rec room and project room. This is where the kids hang out and get creative in any number of ways. We also took our formal dining room, which went unused for two years, and turned it into a resource and computer room. This is where all of our computers are, and all of the resources they need at their fingertips for interest-led pursuits. They can access books on any topic, games, kits, projects, maps, and more. Anything that is not displayed and available here is stored in our two hall closets.

I have had moms tell me that their kids are not creative, so things like this are not necessary for them. I disagree. Every single person is creative in a different way. You could be creative in technology, art, music, engineering, gardening, architecture, mathematics, or any number of areas. The point is that we all function best when we are in an environment that encourages and inspires us to be good at what we do.

We have gone so far as to rearrange our home to better accommodate the various interests of our children. Each of their growth and interests is that important to us. The way we utilize every inch of our home is very intentional.

My children need to be able to access the things that they need. We also want to give them consistent invitations to explore. One such example of this is when we got one of our sons a piano. We initially placed it in the rec room. In this same room were a TV, video game consoles, and toys. It is the most common gathering place in the house. He had a hard time finding an opportunity to practice or try something new on the piano. In between all of the action in the room, it just was not happening as often as he would like. Have you ever tried to make room for something as large as a piano? We had to rearrange our entire resource room just to make it happen for him. This gave him a more attractive invitation to explore.

We have done this with other children as well when it came to finding ways for them to store their creations and tools. We also set up a sewing station for my daughter so that she has a place to cut and create her amazing projects. It is a lot of work to accommodate all six of their needs, but we do what we can to make it happen.

Resources

I am always on the lookout for new resources. It is our goal as parents to provide a resource-rich environment for our kids. I want to create an environment that screams "Check this out," "Isn't this cool?," or "Let's create." In our resource room, I have posters on the wall with encouraging sayings. One of them says, "There are new things to learn all around you." This is exactly why each room (some rooms more than others) has a collection of things that inspire conversation, exploration, and curiosity. Not in a knick-knack kind of way, because I am a clean freak. However, I try to simply design our home where learning opportunities surround them and are not set aside as "learning resources" to only be touched during "learning times" in "learning places."

For instance, I have traveled all over the world. I always bring back things that represent the places I have been, like bibles in the local languages, wood carvings from trees that only grow in that country, locally crafted instruments or games, or art represented from that part of the world. All of these things spark conversations and an opportunity for me to share what I have learned with my children. They can span topics such as wildlife, cuisine, economics, agriculture, culture, music, politics, religion, world history, and more.

"I want to create an environment that screams "Check this out," "Isn't this cool?," or "Let's create.""

This mom is a collector of resources. I use to be so proud of my collection of stuff. It was all beautifully organized by topic in two huge closets. Guess what? They went completely unused. I wasn't purchasing things to stack and hide away. They needed to be utilized.

Finally, I came to a conclusion that I needed to find a way to put the resources I had collected for so long out in front of my kids. They were out of sight, out of mind.

This made my OCD mind spin when I thought about what kind of clutter this would cause. However, they were not benefiting my kids organized and categorized in the closet.

I decided to start creating topical strewing baskets (unforced learning opportunities). Each basket has a collection of resources on the same or a similar topic from different points of view. For instance, a chemistry basket could have a periodic table experiment kit, periodic table puzzle, a laminated card with a list of chemistry websites, a chemistry game, and a few magazines on the topic. I did this with living math resources, writing resources, as well as various types of science.

There are no rules to using the resources in these baskets. They are available in our resource room for free access whenever they want to use them. Sometimes I will pull projects out of them on a theme day and engage the kids with them. For the most part, it is just a way to categorize our resources so that they can find them when needed.

I also purchased a few three-tier rolling carts. My children are very much into creating and making things like crafts, sewing projects, and electronic components. I used one of these rolling carts as a mobile maker space. It includes old toy parts, old electronic pieces and devices for exploration, tools, building kits, idea books, and scraps of all kinds for creativity. I used another three-tier cart to house art supplies and tools. The carts can be rolled anywhere inside or outside for easy usage.

Art

Art is beautiful. It is beautiful because it is an expression of an individual's thought or how they see the world.

Have you taken a trip through the hallways of an elementary school lately? How many times have you seen the exact same picture or project created by thirty different children? You may have a kid that is not into art. Is it possible that their creativity has been stifled due to the expected outcomes?

My goal with my children is personal creative expression. I achieve this by providing an endless supply of tools and materials for them to create without an expected outcome. The beautiful things that they create are so much better than any template or project I could find to duplicate.

I will admit that I had to get rid of my hang-ups of everything being in its place at all times. With six creative kids, I had to extend them grace to create. Yes, they know that they must clean up after themselves and keep their environment tidy, but they are free to get messy in the process. The results are worth it.

One way that we contain the "creative clutter" is by providing each kid with a form of storage for their unfinished and finished projects. Those that do not have space to store things in their own rooms have folders and tubs to store their art, projects, and inventions. If a child has an interest that includes an extensive collection of supplies and tools, we try to find a space for it.

My criteria for quality resources:

- Multiple uses
- Can be used for several children/ages
- Wide open purpose
- Several projects included
- Has all of the materials included for the project/experiment
- Sale price

My favorite resources:

- Building kits
- Science kits
- Electronic kits
- Books, books, and more books
- Hands-on project kits
- Monthly subscriptions (e.g., Universal Yums, Tinker Crate)
- Empty notebooks
- Board/card games

- Maker space supplies

Unschooling on a Budget

By looking at our resources, it may seem like I spend a lot of money. Yes and no. I spend the same as other families, we just have different priorities. While many homeschool families spend hundreds of dollars on curriculum and traditional learning programs, we prioritize other things. We do not use a pre-created or boxed curriculum.

Financial Priorities

- Hands-on kits and supplies/tools
- Diverse home library
- Interest-led lessons/programs
- Sports/classes
- Field trips/travel
- Maximize the use of the library and internet

When purchasing items, I rarely buy something full price unless it will be widely used and enjoyed. I look through used sites like Craig's List and Facebook Marketplace. I peruse garage sales, second-hand stores, going out of business sales, Amazon specials, and Barnes and Noble educator appreciation days.

It takes time to build up a collection of resources that are vast, reliable, timeless, and reusable. My goal has always been to have a wide range of resources to expose them to at all ages. Once you have built that collection, it becomes less and less costly.

Technology and Television

We utilize technology as a tool in our home. There are so many resources that you can access online for free or at minimal cost to help your kids explore different interests.

We only allow internet usage in our family computer lab, and all activity goes to my phone for review. We have a running list of approved websites they can explore. This saves us a lot of money by accessing free and instant information on the web.

"All my kids would do is play video games and watch TV!" I would be wealthy if I had a dollar for each time I have been told this. People assume that technology would be the only choice their child might make if they loosened the reigns.

I believe that your children would surprise you if you gave them the opportunity to make choices. I also think that technology and TV are tools that can be utilized for all kinds of learning opportunities. This is how we deal with technology and television in our home.

Content - What we make available on the TV, gaming system, or computer lines up with our values. This keeps us from the fear of "too much violence" or "inappropriate content."

Options - When you create an environment where there are engaging things to learn and explore all around them, they will be drawn to other things outside of TV and video games.

Parameters - When we see addictive behavior or they display attitudes that we feel came from tech or TV, we review the content and/or have a family tech black-out where we focus on other things. Sometimes it is refreshing for the entire family to unplug.

Safety - Teach your kids about internet safety. Do your due diligence with websites and resources you are unfamiliar with. Get a trustworthy safety software/app for your computers and devices to block out inappropriate content.

Investigate - Don't be so quick to dismiss what your kids are getting out of the video games they play. Play and learning go together.

Get involved - Sit down and play a video game with them. Enter your child's world and seek to understand what they enjoy about the games they play. You would be surprised by the strategy, math, science, and reading that is absorbed during a video game.

Family Computer Lab

As I mentioned, we dismantled the classroom and opted to use our spaces in a way that would better suit our new learning environment. My dream for years was to have a family computer lab. I know it sounds lofty for a family our size and I had no idea how I would do it. With six kids who were getting older and would have the need to investigate and research the things that interested them, I felt this was a necessity.

I love how God makes some of the wildest of our dreams come true. A business in our city had a computer giveaway. They were giving away refurbished computers to the first 250 kids that showed up. Guess who was first in line? Yep! The Sensational Six each got their own computer. Sometimes all you have to have is a vision for something, and everything falls into place.

Now that we have our computer lab, it has taken exploration to an entirely different level. Several kids can be on the computer at one time doing completely different things. Because they are all in the same room, I can easily monitor internet safety and help them all as they need it.

Public Library

The library is also a way to expose your kids to a countless number of topics for free. We get approximately one hundred books a month from our local library, and it expands my children's knowledge in so many areas. We have three criteria whenever we go to the library:

- Books for fun
- Books surrounding their interests
- New ideas, industries, activities to strew

Home Library

Books, books, and more books! Books are a huge deal around here, and they are our most dominant resource. Not all books. Living books. Books that put you in the story and take you on a journey through the eyes of someone who has been there. Books that make a topic come alive. I am very intentional about building a vast home library that spans many genres, styles, biographies, and levels. My kids can be found reading all day just because we put a premium on books.

Field Trips

A large part of our learning is seeing the world and how it works. Of course, we do some of the usual field trips like the zoo, museums, and farms. However, I try to think far outside the box when it comes to the places I expose the kids to. I try to take into account my kids' various interests as well as out-of-the-box excursions that will open their minds to new things and ideas. When my children have experienced new places and processes, I notice it shows up in their art, writing, books they choose, play time, building projects, and inventions. Here are some of our favorite field trips:

- Manufacturing plants
- Chocolate factory tour
- Historical sites
- Maker fairs
- Cultural festivals
- Butterfly exhibits
- Gardens
- Urban farming workshops
- Book binding plant

Learning Outdoors

I cannot stress enough how important it is for our children to spend time outdoors. We need to surround ourselves with fresh air, get exercise, and take in all the beauty that nature has to offer. It is good for the soul.

During the summer months in Michigan, my children spend an average of three hours a day outdoors. This is unstructured play and exploration time.

Nature is an inspiring silent teacher. Get outside! Every topic can be approached from the perspective of nature.

Math, all sciences, art, and endless opportunities for writing and storytelling await your family in the wild.

- Read outside
- Write outside
- Create/draw/paint outside
- Explore the trees, flowers, wildlife

- Investigate math patterns in nature
- Chronicle weather patterns and seasons
- Play

What is Strewing?

As I mentioned earlier, strewing is an unforced and non-coerced way of providing resources without expectations. It is placing things of interest as well as new concepts, activities, books, games, field trips, and websites in their path without an expectation of interest or use. It is simply a soft suggestion placed in their path for consideration.

It is important not to use strewing as a manipulative tool to get your kids to learn something. Children see us coming a mile away when we are trying to turn everything into a lesson instead of allowing it to be a natural learning opportunity.

Pay close attention to your kids. The way they think, the way they choose to learn, and what makes them tick are all clues. This sparks ideas as to what kinds of resources to strew.

As the parent, you operate as a silent partner. Provide the environment, support, and encouragement for exploration and sit back and watch. When and if they choose to explore the item or resource, you are there to assist.

Sometimes I am strewing something random to see if any of the children are interested in it. Other times I am strewing something specific for a particular child based on my observations.

I may put out several games on the table and walk away or maybe start setting up a game and see if anyone would like to join me. I may lay out all of our resources on a topic that I have noticed them mention or engage in and walk away. No force. No expectation. If no one bites, I pack it up and try something else. I have even been surprised many times when I assumed one child would be very interested in an activity or topic and it actually appealed to a different child.

What do I strew?

- Books
- Magazines
- Games
- Field trips
- Classes
- Websites
- Documentaries
- Movies
- Hands-on activities
- Maker space supplies
- Art/craft supplies
- Interest-specific materials (sewing supplies, robotics, sports, etc.)

I have had both success and failure when it comes to strewing. You have to get your emotional attachment to the resource out of the picture. Something that you think your children may be over the moon about may not interest them at all.

I have had times when I have found something that I thought would be the perfect item for one of my children. For example, my oldest son talked about playing the guitar for years. I found an antique acoustic guitar, and I was so excited to give it to him. I could hardly wait. He tinkered on it once in a while for a few weeks and never touched it again. I was offended and admit that I missed the whole point of strewing. I could not make him enjoy the guitar, and he shouldn't have to pretend he loves it to protect my feelings. I eventually picked my lip up off of the floor and let it go.

When a child expresses an interest in something, start with free or inexpensive resources first. The library, online resources, and affordable field trips are an excellent way to test the waters before investing the big bucks. I have learned this the hard way. Once a child has an interest that seems to be getting more profound and more involved, that is when we begin to invest and commit resources to that interest.

I have had more successes when it comes to strewing than I have had failures. One such moment makes me smile just thinking about it. My youngest daughter got an American Girl doll for her tenth birthday last year. She immediately started making doll clothes out of everything she could find. I decided to invest in a beginner sewing machine. It was very basic, but it would be something she could tinker around with, and if she did not show interest, I would be okay with it. Not only did she show interest, but she also made doll clothes, dog clothes, purses, clothes for herself, and clothes for her siblings. This was a win for sure in the strewing department. We recently invested in a quality sewing machine for her to expand her skills and passion in this area. She has also begun to take sewing classes to perfect her craft.

I can think of dozens of these triumphant strewing moments that have taken my children on a journey of exploration into new territories. As I say often, "Exposure ignites a fire." Your kids will find their "thing" once they see it or experience it. My goal is that each of my children will be inspired to explore by the environment that I create.

YouTube Companion

Videos Channel: Karla and the Sensation Six

Videos: Strewing with Success
What is Strewing?
Gameschooling Favorites
Part 1 - Love of the Library
Part 2 - Love of the Library
What about TV and Video Games?
Child-Led Learning Spaces

Chapter 13
Paying Attention

"Let the child be the scriptwriter, the director, and actor in his own play."
— Magda Gerber

When I decided to let my children pursue their interests, I was afraid that I would not see the results that I was seeing everyone talk about. What if it doesn't work for us? What if we're not that kind of family? Am I wasting precious time when I could be teaching them out of a curriculum? Have I been misled? Have I been misinformed? Am I taking an unnecessary detour here?

Setting aside all of my insecurities, I began to look very deeply into what they were choosing to do. I was starting to see with new eyes and perspective. Everyday living became a learning opportunity.

Now most homeschoolers would say, "Oh yes, we learn through life all the time." That is not what I'm talking about. I am talking about literally seeing and responding to learning opportunities all around you, to the point that you have retrained your eye. Things I had never acknowledged as being an opportunity for my children to explore now came to life for me. What used to be a box of Legos became an opportunity to engineer, create, dream, collaborate, and lead.

Paying attention is important for two reasons. First, your children will see that their interests matter to you. Secondarily, the pocket of time may pass if they do not have the proper resources or encouragement to explore that interest.

I can only share so many examples with you here. I'll start with my oldest child and work my way down. These are the things that we began to notice when we started really paying attention.

Social Butterfly (15)
My oldest daughter had struggled in math ever since she was in public school. That struggle continued when we decided to homeschool, and it still ended in tears. I didn't know what to do. I didn't know where to turn, and I looked for answers all around me. There were none. Do you know what we decided to do? We decided to drop all formal math lessons. We agreed that our relationship with our daughter was much more important than her mastering math at that moment. Yes, we knew that there were certain things she needed to know in life and, yes, we planned on exposing her to all of those things. However, our relationship with our daughter was crumbling over math pages.

Soon after abandoning our plans, I happened upon a website that offered free college-level courses. Our daughter had dibble-dabbled in writing poetry and short stories in the past. I thought she could handle the content and assignments. So when she was eleven years old, I signed her up for a college-level poetry course. Why on earth would I sign an eleven-year-old up for a college course? I saw the potential in my daughter. Getting to see her flourish through this course made us realize that her greatness was hidden in plain sight. We almost missed it by pushing her in the opposite direction. I began to see this young lady love literature, love writing, and read voraciously. My daughter got a 98% grade in a college-level poetry course. This was a game-changer for me. I began to see her with new eyes. We were starting to see what God created her to do from a whole new perspective.

"Her greatness was hidden in plain sight. We almost missed it by pushing her in the opposite direction."

I could have pushed and pulled and forced math, but we decided to take another route, and, as a result, we had a breathtaking and delightful outcome.

After taking the course, she continued to write poetry and short stories. She continued to be a voracious reader.

Around February 2013, my daughter brought me a notebook. In this notebook was a book that she had written. When I sat down to read it, I was utterly blown away. She displayed skill, creativity, imagination, culture, history, and science all wrapped up in one story. I was such a proud mom. I really did not want her to stop writing. How could we cultivate this gift in our child?

We decided that we would encourage the self-publishing process to be part of her learning experience. We began down the road of creative writing, editing, publishing, marketing, sales, business, design, and everything else that comes with this experience. Not to mention the geography, history, language, and cultural background of all the countries she studied to bring her books to life.

She has loved it. We began to see a whole new person and confidence beaming from her that we had never seen before. She found her thing. This was when her gift and passion took on a whole new form.

Her passion for writing turned into a desire to pursue scriptwriting and film production. Paying attention was vital at this pivotal moment. I used to ask myself why all of her books were full of so much dialogue, kind of like a play or a movie. It was a clue of bigger things to come. We signed her up for film camp at an excellent college in our area. This exposed her to screenwriting skills, location scouting, set design, cinematography, lighting, audio, casting of characters, production, camera/filming skills, and editing. Following this camp, she had the opportunity to begin serving in the media and film department at our church.

By following her two passions of writing and film, she was exposed to an array of skills that she probably would not have touched the surface of in a traditional learning environment. Encouraging her to write and publish her books is not an attempt to make her the next child genius you see on the news, nor is it to make her a teen millionaire. It is about her learning, growing, and getting hands-on experience in an area of interest. Did she learn, improve, make mistakes, and recover? That is what is important to us.

Letting go of our expectations and what we thought she needed to do brought about a whole new fire. We let go, and as a result, she flourished. Today, my daughter is a fifteen-year-old author of three self-published books and is in the process of writing her fourth. Her goal before her eighteenth birthday is to publish several books. This was not our goal for her. This was her goal for herself. If at any time she decided to change her mind, we would support her.

We are so happy that we did what we thought was right and, as a result, our daughter is loving life, and her joy of learning has returned.

My observation over time is that she needed space to exercise her talents without preconceived guidelines. The way she learns is by doing. She is a creative thinker with an abundance of ideas that require passionate expression.

Brain (14)
He always struggled in the area of writing. I pushed and forced him to do book reports and other writing assignments, and it was like pulling teeth. It was definitely an area of contention between us. Like his sister, I decided that we needed to stop. When I stopped forcing him to write what I wanted him to write, he began writing on his own.

He writes excellent fictional stories. What stood out most to me is that he started to write instructional materials on aviation and engineering processes of random things. If I had not paid attention to this, I would have continued to push to no avail. Now he willingly writes about his passion.

At the age of ten, we celebrated his birthday at the Air Zoo. The Air Zoo is a museum for historical, scientific, and hands-on experiences in aviation. Wow, was he turned on fast. At that point he began to express a keen interest in aviation. I started to look for every book and website I could find. It was not long before I had exhausted all the resources I knew of. He became bored and restless. He wanted more.

I started asking around to find programs that would allow him to experience hands-on learning in this particular area. I thought it would be a long shot to find anyone who was going to let a child his age actually fly.

I finally talked to the right people. They led me to a program right here in our city. He started ground school, which is the educational portion of the program, in the fall of 2016. He also co-pilots a plane every month with a private instructor. He is now going into his third year in this program. He will take his exam to become a licensed pilot in a couple of years.

This has come with a sacrifice of time, effort, and money, but it is something that he is passionate about. We are so excited for where this will lead him. Getting a pilot's license for him is only the first step in what he desires to do in the field of aviation. He's interested in avionics, aviation mechanics, commercial airlines, and entrepreneurship.

Before entering college, his goal is to have both his pilot's license and his avionics certification. He is on track to do both as a result of his own hard work and vision for his future.

As his parents, we are so happy that we paid attention to his needs and developed an environment where he can spend the bulk of his time on the things that he loves. My observation and conclusions after watching him over time are that my son loves formalized bodies of knowledge and factual data. He wants to read about it, see it, and prove it out. He wants to express his expertise to anyone who will listen and hear different viewpoints on the same topics.

Thunderbolt (12)

This kid is the perfect unschooler. He was the three-year-old I told you about when we first started homeschooling that was not trying to hear any of it. From the very beginning, he was his own person and danced to the beat of his own drum. Admittedly, that is what everyone loves so much about him. He is passionate, charismatic, and bold about his interests. He seeks knowledge and digs for explanations until he reaches an answer. Trying to homeschool him traditionally was a disaster. He had to have his freedom to roam, explore, and come to conclusions on his own. Transitioning to interest-led learning was perfect for him.

Paying attention to his needs was so important. He began spending hours at a time researching historical events, wars, and world cultures. Then it turned into memorizing all the battles within the wars, significant leaders, and how different countries were connected to world events. That interest began four years ago. It is still going strong today. He also started studying weather patterns and watching endless playlists on natural disasters. Both of these areas have become his most significant areas of interests.

He also loves video games and creating short films. He has a special gift to understand technology and technical systems. This kid is a natural born leader. Just recently he was a part of a coding and business leadership camp that allowed him to exercise his creative skills in a group forum.

We are not sure where all of his interests will lead, but we highlight all of them and continuously strew resources and opportunities for him to strengthen every area. Over time, I have seen him learn best from being entirely left alone. He is also a moving learner, meaning he learns best when in action. He likes to come to his own conclusions, find his own resources, and immerse himself in information for long periods of time. He emerges with a full body of knowledge and conclusions that baffle us every day.

Ninja Princess (11)
This child has both a scientific and artistic bent. As early as seven years old, she showed a strong desire for knowledge about the human body. Not just memorizing the systems or organs, but an intense need to see real footage of surgeries. At that age, she would spend hours watching actual C-sections, brain surgeries, heart transplants, and anything that had to do with the human body. We began to strew lots of medical terminology resources, surgery game apps, books, board games, field trips, and anything we could think of to feed her curiosity in this area.

Her newest interests include all types of dance. She has also become immersed in sewing and fashion design. She is sewing her own clothes and accessories with passion and skill. She also enjoys inventing gadgets, art, and crafting.

This is why paying attention is so important. If you are not aware of what makes your kids tick, you will miss the opportunity to invest in and encourage their interests.

Seeing her in action over the years makes me smile. She is a doer and a tester. Everything she learns is from building, testing, and improving processes. Her need for freedom in her day is paramount. She does not like unnecessary time wasters and prefers to get straight to the action. We look forward to seeing how her scientific and artistic worlds collide.

Quiet Storm (10)
Sometimes you will have a child who is less vocal in a sea of children that are very expressive. This is where paying close attention is crucial. For a very long time, I could not quite put my finger on his interests. It frustrated me to no end. He would follow his twelve-year-old brother and engage in whatever he was doing. This made it increasingly hard to see what made him tick.

Sitting down with him and having a conversation helped me home in on what has always been there. He loves to draw. He loves science, drawing, reading, and playing piano. These are things that have surfaced from time to time. They were not prominent because he is a more subdued personality. We began buying him science and art books, and he started doing art tutorials on YouTube. He just started piano and is loving it. He was a hard nut to crack, but Mommy has gotten to the bottom of his learning needs.

He is a watcher. He will study and watch people, processes, and systems for a while before trying it. When he finally dives in, it is like he has been doing it forever. He needs me to advocate for his interests. Being less aggressive and vocal than his other siblings, he will naturally dive into their interests with them and forget about his own. I intentionally redirect him to the things he loves to help him balance that out. He recently began piano lessons. I know with the right exposure and encouragement, he will do very well at whatever he chooses to pursue.

If you have a child who is more laid back, you have to press in to figure out what they love and expose them to as many things as possible to help them figure it out.

Boss (9)
It is not easy being the baby of the family. Many times you are overshadowed by everyone else. Not this kid. He is bold, tenacious, and knows what he wants.

For as long as I can remember, he has wanted to be a police officer or detective. He is passionate about forensic sciences, detective strategies, law, and justice.

These themes play out in every imaginary scenario he engages in, every video game he plays, and books he chooses to read. He has quite a brilliant engineering mind. My little guy is also a tester. He is a gadget maker and creator of amazing things. He loves to improve systems and processes. He becomes fully engaged in a project that could last days before he comes up for air. He is not one to openly share his intelligence but always surprises us with his random wisdom and ideas that are baffling. We continually encourage his interests as he gets older and homes in on what he wants to pursue.

Why did I share these things with you? I wanted to share these details about my children because these are things that I never noticed or even acknowledged before we began unschooling. I was too busy trying to check off the scope and sequence list. My focus was on someone else's plan instead of on my children and what makes each of them unique and valuable.

It never even occurred to me to pay attention to the things that make them tick. They were all clues to what and how they learn. They were also clues as to what they needed from me as a supporter of their learning. I can confidently say that I know my children.

I encourage you to step back and watch your children. Pay attention to the things they say, do, and choose.

Intentionally look at them with new eyes. You will see things you have never seen before. These will be the clues to help them explore the world around them and become all that God called them to be.

Chapter 14
Exposure Ignites Fires

"Play is not only our creative drive, it's a fundamental way of learning."
— David Elkind

What if my children don't have a passion? Have no fear. Everyone has a passion. Many go through their lives without realizing it because they have never been exposed to it. I truly believe that exposure ignites fires. If your child does not have a passion or dominant interest, it is because they have not seen it, touched it, or experienced it yet. Once they do, you will know. It will be undeniable.

Your job is to expose your kids to a wide range of people, places, things, and topics in a variety of ways. Seeing, hearing, and experiencing multiple industries, lines of work, professional environments, and skill sets will open their eyes to so many opportunities and help them home in on their interests. This not only helps them find their "thing," but it also helps your child figure out areas that are *not* of interest to him or her.

What if they change their mind? What if we spend time, energy, and money on something and they decide to go in a different direction? Great news! No amount of time, effort, or money spent on your child's interest is wasted. It is all leading somewhere. The skill sets, knowledge, and confidence they gain from whatever they pursue will only add to their future endeavors.

Will it be wasted time if my daughter wrote several books before she turned eighteen, even if she decided that she wants to do something completely different? The skills she developed writing, editing, speaking, designing, publishing, marketing, and gaining business skills will serve her in any direction she chooses.

Will having a pilot's license at seventeen be useless if my son goes in a different direction? What if he spends four years in this aviation program and decides that he wants to pursue something else? The experience he has had in aviation, science, navigation, geography, safety, mechanical maintenance, and leadership will still serve him in his future career.

Everything they learn will ultimately benefit them in the long run, no matter what direction they choose. Don't belittle a child's interest. Whether your child is four or seventeen, downplaying their interest can knock the wind out of their sails. It may seem futile or insignificant to you. Just be there, engage, and supply resources on their level. Some interests may pass and others may last years; others may lead to their life's work. They are all important.

"If your child does not have a passion or dominant interest, it is because they have not seen it, touched it, or experienced it yet."

What if my kid is unmotivated?

I don't believe in unmotivated learners. However, I do believe in uninspired learners. There is something that makes your child tick. Inspiration over time will help them discover their "thing." A heart to heart conversation with them will reveal what is going on. This will allow you to help them get out of a slump.

A perfect example of this is my oldest son. I told you that he had the hardest time adjusting to unschooling out of all of the kids. What looked like laziness, lack of motivation, and rebellion to me was actually confusion. He could not learn what he desired to learn through the avenues I was providing for him. He wanted online classes and loves textbooks. I wanted him to be free and learn like his siblings and he wanted something different. Just because he wished to have resources in a traditional form does not mean he is not an unschooler. He decides what he wants to explore, when he wants to study it, and how. I facilitate that and provide the resources.

I had mistaken his frustration for lack of motivation. Today, he spends his day doing both traditional and hands-on learning. He is very comfortable with his own unique approach. When he was finally exposed to the right resources and things he loved, that fire was lit!

As parents, we cannot get discouraged when our kids find their "thing" in their twenties instead of their teens. Some of us are still discovering who we are. Don't put constant pressure on your kids to have a complete vision for the next fifty years of their life. Pushing and fussing show your frustration and in turn this causes them to shut down.

Relax! Exposure, exposure, exposure! This will help guide them and give them enough experiences to broaden their horizons now and in the future. One of my favorite books on the topic is *Unschooling Rules* by Clark Aldrich. He has a chapter called "Expose More, Teach Less" that focuses on the importance of self-directed learning. This book opened my eyes to the significance of exposure.

If God created every single person as an individual with unique gifts and callings, then we all have a passion. It may not be evident, that does not mean it is non-existent. Exposure ignites a fire. When you expose your children to the world around them in a variety of ways, that world opens up, and their interests take center stage.

"To develop a complete mind, study the science of art; study the art of science. Learn how to see. Realize that everything connects to everything else."
— Leonardo de Vinci

Why do we separate topics? Everything is connected. Before the current education system was created unschooling was the norm. People learned at home or in the field in hands-on ways. Once we begin to separate learning into topics, it fails to show our children how everything connects. You cannot separate numbers from the very areas in life to which they apply. It causes the learning to be fragmented and useless in the minds of children. That is why we have so many who say, "I will never use this math in the real world." They were taught that math was separate from art, science, and history. It is a part of every area of our lives. The kind of math they would pursue depends on their direction in life.

My goal is holistic learning, an environment that helps my kids connect the dots between art, math, science, geography, and history. I want my children to have a view of the world that can see the science in music and dance. When you remove the barriers of subjects or separate topics, then you expose them to a world that is interwoven, connected, and fluid.

YouTube Companion Video
Channel: Karla and the Sensational Six
Video: Exposure Ignites Fire

SAMPLE DOCUMENT

"Mom, I'm Bored."

- Read a good book
- Read to a sibling
- Explore outdoors, go for a walk, have a picnic
- Do a science experiment
- Do a lapbook
- Create an artistic masterpiece/craft
- Help out around the house
- Build something out of new materials
- Watch a movie/documentary, show, or DVD
- Play a card/board game
- Do a puzzle
- Finish an incomplete project
- Write a poem or story
- Practice your sport, instrument, skill
- Mind Bender games
- Snap Circuits/Maker Space Project
- Engineering kits
- Lego challenge
- Dance challenge
- Research something you want to learn about
- Cook or bake something yummy
- Ride your bike
- Invent something

Chapter 15
Rabbit Trails

"The children are the curriculum."

— Lisa Murphy

Following rabbit trails gets my adrenaline pumping. There is something about seeing bells and whistles go off when my kids discover something new.

I was not always like this. Being the systematic and orderly thinker that I am, rabbit trails used to upset me. I had a plan and strategy to get all the boxes checked off, and any deviation was the enemy of my progress. Notice how I said "*my* progress." I was so absorbed by what I wanted to accomplish that I was not paying much attention to my kids' needs and interests.

Timing

Now our days are full of rabbit trails. It can seem chaotic, but there really is a rhythm to it. Once it becomes a regular part of your day, you expect it and you open yourself up to it. It is easy to be so tunnel focused that we miss out on essential windows of opportunity. These opportunities don't always present themselves again.

There are times when I feel like I am hanging upside down from the ceiling when my kids ask the most profound questions. I could get frustrated and wave them off to go do something else. Instead, I either stop what I am doing, if it is not imperative, or I tell them to write it down and remind me to jump into that topic with them. I try not to wait too long between their initial curiosity and my help. I don't want them to miss the opportunity to learn something new.

I have to intentionally choose to be flexible. If we push our kids off when they want our help in exploring a topic, then they begin to feel their interests are not significant. How unfortunate that would be.

Distracted Kids

Our kids are sponges. Sometimes we label daydreamers or children with attention deficits unfairly. That very thing can be used as an opportunity for the most fantastic rabbit trails. We still work to help them with their struggles. It just means we take what is happening naturally and have some fun with it. Your child will appreciate it.

I have a child who seems distracted to others. However, he retains more when he is duly occupied. Because I understand that, I make sure that I provide things for him to do simultaneously while reading aloud or while doing other auditory activities.

Flexibility

If you do not value rabbit trails, you will view them as a distraction or annoyance instead of acknowledging them as meaningful learning. Be flexible and allow your kids to flow and explore a topic for however long and deep they desire.

In this day of technology with the world at our fingertips, it is easy to pause a moment and help your kid get answers. You can crack a code that unleashes an entirely new topic.

Multi-faceted

Every possible topic you can think of is multi-faceted. This means that you can dig deeper and branch off into any number of directions. The learning opportunities from that initial curiosity are limitless.

One thing leads to another, and another, and before you know it, you and your child have jumped head first into a new body of knowledge. It may not be planned or on your agenda for the day. That does not mean that it is not meaningful learning.

"If you do not value rabbit trails, you will view them as a distraction or annoyance instead of acknowledging them as meaningful learning."

Books

We are read-a-holics. We love books! A perfect example of a rabbit trail happens when a child is exposed to a good book. One of my sons read a simple book on Greece around the time that he became a fluent reader. He immediately started asking questions. He found it on the map. He studied what kind of food they eat and grow.

This led him to the climate and body of water that surrounds the country. He wanted to know what their houses look like and what the language sounds like. In one afternoon, he studied everything he could about Greece. Three years later, he is so passionate about the country that he cannot wait to visit. It all started with one book he picked up in our home library.

Much of what he wanted to know, he needed help finding. I am sure that I could have found any number of things to occupy my attention at that moment. I had to be flexible enough to indulge his curiosity and find resources to help him research.

Survival

Sometimes a rabbit trail is started by one child, and then it catches fire. Before you know it, the whole family is diving into the topic.

Such an example happened recently. My twelve-year-old son is passionate about survivalist strategies. One day he found a new survival show that he binge-watched for weeks. As he got into them, the rest of the kids began to gain interest as well. Then Dad and I started to enjoy the shows with them.

This interest took so many turns and detours that it became a survivalist learning carnival. Before long, the kids were asking for tools and wood. They were carving bows and arrows and learning what kinds of materials make fire (with oversight). It led to wanting to forage for natural food, which led to identifying edible and non-edible plants. That then led to many of my children experimenting with gardening.

They built forts out of sticks from the woods near our home. They planted seeds. They studied different kinds of terrain and discussed how to survive as they recalled the shows they watched. We even had survival quiz bowl games at the dinner table.

This went on and on for about three weeks. For some of the kids, it was a brief pause to learn something new. For others, it sparked new interests and has lasted. Was this inconvenient? Very much so. Dad and I had to be available to teach them how to use the tools they needed for their impromptu projects. They asked for help and suggestions when they got stumped. We even allowed them to use household items, which we never would have done before. This was one of the most delightful learning experiences we have engaged in as a family; almost everyone enjoyed the same thing.

Geography and History

Our favorite subscription kit is Universal Yums. It is a monthly subscription that sends a box of twelve treats from a different country each month. They come with a trivia and history book about the nation as well.

My kids get so excited when that blue and white box shows up. As we delve into our box, it has led us to discover agriculture in that part of the world based on the treats we are enjoying. Some of the goodies have historical significance and lead us to dig into things we never would have thought to explore. What starts as a quick yummy treat turns out to be a two-hour investigation into an entirely different country led by my kids' curiosity. What an exciting way to explore the world without ever touching a world history textbook.

Animal Rescues

My kids love nature and wildlife. The summertime brings so much fun and wonder. We have become a rescue haven for small animals. Sometimes my kids are not necessarily rescuing as much as they are exploring and studying the little creatures.

There was the time our neighbor asks us to bat-sit. You read that right. She rescued a baby bat and had to work the next day. We were to keep him safe and have fun studying him until she could get him to a wildlife shelter. This experience took us on a rabbit trail that we never expected. It was winter. We could not figure out why he was outside during that time of the year. This led us to investigate weather patterns and the migration patterns of bats. That led us to study what they need to stay alive and why so many were dying all over our state. We are happy to say he made it to the rescue center and was released successfully.

The same thing happened with a baby rabbit that my kids found in a field near our home. They watched it from afar for a long time before realizing that the mommy rabbit was not coming back. They created a habitat and researched what to feed him. After a full day of enjoying our new buddy, our neighbor came to get him and take him to a rescue center. We did consider keeping the rabbit, but we have a hunting dog that would not have taken kindly to the rabbit's presence.

This same story can be repeated with toads and a turtle the boys rescued from the road, which they released after studying. Building habitats and nursing animals back to health while learning all we can about them is par for the course around here. We never planned this. They were hiccups in the middle of a day that I planned on doing something else. Yet, the detour was an unforgettable one. What they learned was sought out by them because of their interest.

Money
I recently had dinner with my friend Jill. She was so excited to tell me about a rabbit trail that had transpired in her home the previous week. It has been her goal to embrace interest-led learning for her homeschoolers.

Her Story:
"It all began as a chemistry assignment. My seventeen-year-old son was working through a Chemistry 101 curriculum, and the chapter was dealing with the various metals used in coins.

As he was working through the assignment, he asked me if coins were still made from bronze and silver. Instead of answering, I encouraged him to look for the answer himself.

He spent a long time learning while stopping along the way to tell me a fact or two about coins, materials used and the meaning of the letters, "D," "S," or "P" on them.

My twelve-year-old daughter was listening to all the facts and heard about the coin that was worth a lot of money. She asked if we could look through the vacation jar. Soon all three of us were going through every coin jar in the house to find a 1943 penny. It was made from a different material which made it weigh less.

Suddenly, my son found a 1943 penny! We freaked out and shared what we would do with the money if it really were the coin. My son pulled out the kitchen scale and decided to compare the weight of the coin to another penny and did more research to see what it looked like.

It turned out that it was not THE 1943 penny that was worth thousands of dollars. But the experience was priceless. We learned about the history and value of money, precious metals, U.S. Mint locations, how coins are made with several elements, research skills, and more!"

Jill wanted to meet to get ideas on implementing interest-led learning in her homeschool. When she told me about this fantastic rabbit trail, I got so excited. Jill was doing all the right things. What if she just answered his questions or ignored his curiosity altogether? What if she did not engage in his learning or allow her daughter to be a part of the hunt? This could have gone an entirely different way. Instead, she participated, encouraged, and became curious with him. This allowed it to be a joint learning experience. One thing led to another, then another. Inspired learning!

It is easy to hand your child a curriculum and check off assignments on a list. It takes flexibility and priority to say, "Let's follow this trail, however long it takes and wherever it leads us." These are the moments that lead to meaningful and inspired learning. They are the moments your children will remember – that day when you dropped everything and dove into something that was important to them. Unschooling households operate like this on a daily basis. This is a way of life.

Most days are entirely random, where all six of my kids want to explore something entirely different and want me to themselves. I slowly make my way around the house to add suggestions, give resources, follow rabbit trails, or answer their questions. The older kids are more versed in following those trails without much help, and I am available when needed. Others need guidance depending on the subject matter or resources necessary to go deeper.

Part 3: Walking It Out

Chapter 16
Unschooling Littles
(2-7 years old)

"Kids don't need more toys, they need more adventures!"

— Sarah Mueller

These are the wonder years! Everything is a new experience and worthy of investigation. Little ones are touching, smelling, hearing, and tasting everything to figure out this great big world. They need to be given the freedom to explore without hard guidelines and formal lessons.

There is nothing more perplexing to me than seeing a mom on a frenzied quest to find a curriculum for her two-year-old. No matter how advanced, gifted, or talented the toddler presents, the child needs to have the freedom to explore their world without force and memorizing facts.

Even adults learn through play. We underestimate the power and significance of play. The younger years are all about exploration, wonder, and the delight of learning.

Creating an alluring environment of sights, sounds, tastes, textures, and relationships will give your child an array of things to learn and do.

"Play gives children a chance to practice what they are learning."
— Fred Rogers

In our home, we spend these very early years making sure that our children understand the world around them. We focus on the relationship, our values, and learning through life. Keeping them at my side and teaching by example always took us down fantastic rabbit trails into conversations and experiences that I never could have planned. Our classroom was the kitchen, nature, grocery stores, parks, field trips, and life.

I encourage reading voraciously to your children. At this age, reading about a wide range of topics allows adventures to take you into new territories. The most consistent thing that we did during this age was read.

Everything that my children will ever want to know may be in a book. I tried to instill a passion for books very early.

We played audio books and stimulating DVDs in the background as they played and did craft projects of their choosing. You would be surprised how much a child retains when they are in a stimulating environment that does not force learning, but makes it available.

I utilized stations a lot when they were younger. I would arrange activities throughout the home that exercised different skills and appealed to a variety of senses. Due to the short attention span of my little ones, I made sure each station was something that could be enjoyed that did not take a long time. They were free to move about and test each station at their own pace. Sometimes they would want to spend a long time on one and had no interest in others. The stations ranged in complexity and topic based on the age and interests of my children. Much of their foundation for reading and creativity came from the early years of relaxed and free exploration.

Reading

Five out of my six children were self-taught readers. I did not use a curriculum or reading program for them at all. I did not pressure them to read by a certain age or get scared when they were not reading like the neighbor's kids.

My goal was for my children to love reading. I wanted it to be something they enjoyed and not something that was forced upon them. We allowed them to develop at their own pace, and it was different for each child. I have children who started reading at four, seven, and even nine years old.

We surround them with books. They see us read and value books. We read to them regularly about a wide variety of topics and faraway places. Surrounding them with an atmosphere that values books and information drove them to begin trying themselves. Once they decided they wanted to read, we spent more time doing it with them – helping their skills to grow and improve.

Other ways that we encouraged reading was adding labels to household items all over the house, TV captions, cooking, and computer games. At this age, I believe formal lessons can stifle a love of learning. It places an idea in the child's mind that play and learning are opposites. Play is the work of childhood.

YouTube Companion Videos
Channel: Karla and the Sensational Six
Videos:
How do Unschoolers/Interest-Led Learners Learn to Read?
How do Unschoolers/Interest-Led Learners Learn Math?

Chapter 17
Unschooling Middles
(8-12 years old)

"No desks, no walls, no textbooks. Just living and learning well." — Karla Marie Williams

This is the testing and experimenting age. Kids tend to find themselves trying all kinds of new things. They test the waters and find out what they enjoy as well as those they do not. They need to be able to experiment with new activities, sports, classes, and programs, even if they don't master them. It helps them to know themselves and what things they may want to continue.

Not every child is confident in their interests at this age. However, they have established some of the things they like and do not like. Most people think that unschooling is cute for younger children, yet they feel older kids need a more structured or systematic learning approach. They want to see things like reading, writing, and math covered out of fear that a child will not choose to learn them on their own. I genuinely believe that any child at any age can benefit from unschooling.

Theme Days
We utilize theme days for this age group the most, exposing them to a wide variety of topics, careers, and industries. It gets their juices flowing and allows me to see what really

makes them tick. You can read more about our theme days in our DITL chapter. Our theme days are very short, hands-on, and engaging projects to enhance the skills they will be utilizing as they follow their interests. Reading, writing, and researching the things they love becomes a natural process they initiate in their daily life.

This age is the time when I do the most strewing to provide a wide variety of hands-on experiences. They begin to make sense of things around them and how they fit into the world. They start to ask more in-depth questions and seek out more detailed answers.

I have noticed the middle years have been a crucial time for my children. This is the time when we read and watch a lot of documentaries about the things they find fascinating.

"We can best help children learn, not by deciding what we think they should learn and thinking about ingenious ways to teach it to them, but by making the world as far as we can, accessible to them, paying serious attention to what they do, answering their questions – if they have any – and helping them explore the things they are most interested in."
— John Holt

This is the beginning of the investment stage. It is the ground-testing phase where you pay close attention to what your kids are choosing to do. Find as many opportunities for them to experiment, test, and perfect skills in those areas as you can. We don't push or solidify any interest at any age. We just pay attention to the clues of their choices, gifts, and talents.

I think that we would find that children are very good at seeking out what works best for them. They probably have three or four things that they are the most interested in at this age.

"At this age, it is imperative that you reach far and wide for as many opportunities as possible for each of your child's most pronounced interests."

I currently have four children in this age group. Unschooling at this stage can be all over the place. You cannot get frustrated by their many interests. You may wonder which one will turn into their life's work – maybe all of them, or perhaps none of them. Our goal is not to estimate or measure the outcome of their lives, but for them to feel their way with support and encouragement as they figure it out for themselves.

At this age, it is imperative that you reach far and wide for as many opportunities as possible for each of your child's most pronounced interests. If they are highly interested in three major areas, even if they are unconnected, find ways for them to experience hands-on learning in all three areas. This will help them to narrow things down and perfect what they care the most about.

Chapter 18
Unschooling Teens
Age (13+)

"Treat a child as though he already is the person he's capable of becoming."
— Haim Ginott

The teen years are for real-world execution. Not all kids know what they want to do with the rest of their lives as teenagers. However, many do. They at least have an idea of the industry, passion, or problem they want to solve in their world. This is the age when we search high and low for real-world opportunities for them. Not just reading about it, watching a documentary, or a field trip – actual execution and on-the-job training. We encourage them to take on real-world roles as they perfect skills and ideas that lead to their ultimate goals.

We want to give them a head start into the areas they wish to pursue. I do not believe that kids have to wait to pursue their dreams. If a child is confident in their direction, why wait?

This may or may not include college. I will not accept the idea that college or a traditional road is the only way for our children to accomplish God's plan for their lives. It may include entrepreneurship, trade expertise, travel, or entering the workforce in an area of interest. Our only expectation is that they work toward the goals they have set for themselves in some way, shape, or form. How they do it is up to them.

By the time my children are the age of most high schoolers, they have usually identified one or two things that really make them come alive. That may not be for every child, in which case you would continue to expose them to a wide variety of experiences until they find their "thing."

I honestly believe that children should have the ability to test the waters and get their hands wet in areas the world generally reserves for adulthood.

As I have said in previous chapters, we do not lock our children into anything. If they decide they want to change their direction, that is their choice. Nothing they have experienced or mastered is wasted time, energy, or money.

Interest-led learning during the teen years can look more traditional for one child and more unschooly for another. It depends on what their desired path may require. An example of this is the stark contrast between my oldest two children, who are teenagers.

When my daughter decided that writing was her passion, we decided to allow her to learn through self- publishing her books. Why should she wait to be an author? Through this process, she is learning about creative writing, editing, formatting, accounting and inventory, public speaking, sales, social media, marketing, and much more. Her one passion led to an array of learning experiences. Based on her path, our math focus has been on consumer math and business math, which we expose to her in hands-on and creative ways. She is considering a small film college in our region for screenwriting and producing. There are also other options that she is weighing outside of the pursuit of college. We are confident that she will succeed no matter which route she takes.

Her Unschooling Teen Years

Her teen years are filled with flexibility. She has a wide range of experiences and has learned a lot of things that will benefit her future endeavors as an author and filmmaker. The bulk of her time is spent doing these activities, but it is not limited to this list.

- She spends the bulk of her time reading a variety of genres, mainly history, biographies, and historical fiction.
- Writing, editing, and publishing her books. Her goal is to write several by age 18.
- She chooses hands-on math projects and consumer math activity books.
- Fencing is her sport of choice.
- She also enjoys investigating environmental science and forensics when she has free time.
- She has and will attend several camps and seminars on film making.
- She has taken multiple online classes on creative writing, history/government, and social sciences upon her request.

- She has attended several writer's workshops/conferences.
- She has spent time doing light gardening for neighbors, as well as testing her own hand at growing food.
- She is an apprentice in the media and film department at church.
- She spends time planning and learning how to run a non-profit to aid her work in Haiti in the future.

"Nothing they have experienced or mastered is wasted time, energy, or money.

My oldest son is very particular about his dreams and goals for himself in the field of aviation. His teen years are going to look very different from his sister's. To pursue the things he wants to do, there are licenses, certifications, and levels he will have to master in some traditional subjects like math and science.

When my son decided that his first goal in the aviation industry was to get his private pilot's license, we went on the hunt for a program that would let him do it now. Why should he wait until he is an adult to fly a plane? He also wants to explore other areas of aviation. By the time he is ready to launch into the world, he will have two licenses that most people wait until they are an adult to pursue. He will have many choices ahead of him: college, continue to get more trade licenses, or work utilizing the two licenses he has already obtained. He has his sights set on one of the highest-ranked aviation colleges in the nation. Unschoolers do go to college if they choose.

His Unschooling Teen Years

Even though his teen years may look a bit traditional, it is all by choice. All of the things he chooses to explore will give him plenty of leverage to pursue his dreams. That list includes, but is not limited to, the items below.

- He challenges himself to go as high as he can in mathematics at his pace.

- He is passionate about physics and chemistry and spends time reading about them, taking online classes, and doing labs.

- He attends flight ground school and co-pilots a plane every month with a goal of receiving his private pilot's license at 17. He studies all aspects of aviation and aerospace continually.

- He studies historical economics, which is a shared passion with his dad. They read and discuss the topics.

- He does a lot of reading and research on business. Entrepreneurship is a goal of his.

- He enjoys dismantling things and figuring things out, so he is always in the middle of some kind of project.

- Technical writing about aviation and flight seem to excite him.

- He is an apprentice under a master gardener.

- He has taken a couple of online science courses in food science.

- He is learning to plant his own above-ground vegetable garden.

- He will be spending two years (ages 16/17) studying Avionics (aviation electronics) for a certification.

- He has attended two aviation camps.

The kinds of resources my teens utilize, the type of things they learn, and how they learn it may be completely different. All of the classes they take, the resources they use, and the activities they take part in are by their own choice. They tell us what they want to do and together we investigate the road that will help them get there. Even if they have to do something challenging to reach their goal, they do it because they want it, not because we force them.

There may be a day when they accomplish nothing on this list and other days when they tackle many of these self-inspired areas, or something new. What is important is that they are working toward something they want on their own timeline in their own way. Over the next two years, I am confident that many things will be added to this list as they delve deeper into their passions and gain other interests.

They choose what areas interest them and spend four years investigating, experimenting, and mastering those areas. Some things they may not continue and others they completely immerse themselves in. For example, my son is spending four years learning all he can learn about chemistry and physics, at his pace. My daughter has spent the bulk of her time writing and studying literature, as well as taking several classes on writing. This is what she loves!

Mentorship

Finding mentors, apprenticeships, trade schools, and hands-on learning opportunities is our priority for teens. I am continually looking for people that do what my kids desire to do. I love that my children are experiencing an element of their dreams and are already doing things that they love.

My favorite website for unschooling teens is www.unschoolrules.com. On this site, you can get samples of what a high school-aged unschooler's plan can look like. She also shares transcript examples. It is an excellent resource.

YouTube Companion Videos
Channel: Karla and the Sensational Six
Videos:
Interest-Led Learning- The High School Years - Part 1
Interest-Led Learning- The High School Years - Part 2
Interest-Led Learning- The High School Years - Part 3

Chapter 19
Read, Write, and the 4-Letter Word

"The way we teach math is all wrong. The reason why math is hard to understand is that it is taught without context."
— Susan Terry, For the Love of Learning Podcast #40

The 3Rs! Every prospective unschooler's extreme fear. This is the number one thing that makes or breaks their decision to follow this path or not.

We have been taught that these things are deal breakers or non-negotiable in formalized education. They have to be taught or they are not valid. It takes a real paradigm shift to understand how these same three things can be learned just by living.

Reading
As the mom of five self-taught readers, and a sixth following right behind, it would take a miracle for you to convince me that reading is something that needs to be formally taught. Providing the right atmosphere and resources will encourage a love of reading without any force at all. A child may need accommodations if a challenge is detected.

In my opinion, the most important skill an unschooler can have is reading. Once a child can read, nothing is hidden from them.

As parents, we qualify reading as if one type of reading is more important than another. The goal is that reading takes place and that the skill increases as they grow and learn. Reading for fun is just as valuable as other reading. Don't get me wrong, I am very particular about the appropriateness of my children's reading choices. However, I give lots of room to choose within our parameters. My kids' favorite things to read are biographies, science fiction, fantasy, historical fiction, interest-related books, and random fact books. The very practice of the skill exercises the mind and opens up our child's world to new things. There are many ways to encourage reading by using life as their teacher. The opportunities are endless.

- Billboards
- Labels
- Signs
- Brochures
- Magazines
- Books of all kinds
- TV captions
- Movie credits
- Games
- Video games
- Recipes
- Project instructions

We have a daily quiet reading time where we shut down all tech and TVs and read in the evening before bed. This happens more during the winter months than in the summer. They read to each other, to themselves, or to us.

Often, I will read aloud or play an audio book while the entire household is engaged in quiet activities. This is one of our favorite things to do on a slow or rainy day. Dad may be reading to himself, the big kids may be writing or doing something on the computer, and the younger four may be painting or building something creative while I read. We will discuss the book together and share perspectives. It is definitely one of my favorite things about being home with my kids. Even the dog curls up and enjoys our family reading time.

Words are everywhere! Continue to encourage and challenge them on new levels of reading and watch them astonish you.

Writing

We live in a technological age. Even still, writing is essential. Does it require formal teaching? More than anything, it requires creativity and risk-taking. The "rules" of writing can be learned as they explore the skill and create bodies of work along the way. There are unlimited opportunities to write every day.

Focusing more on content and creativity in writing is crucial to develop a love for it. When we focus on skill and technicality too early, we kill the enjoyment before we get started. Skill will develop in time.

Throughout the year we give all six of our children blank notebooks. No rules. No stipulations. Our only requirement is that they fill them up with words. How they use them is as unique as the child. One of these notebooks turned out to be my oldest daughter's first self-published book. You can encourage some of these activities that will help them to develop a voice and style of writing all their own.

- Diary
- Poetry
- Nature journals
- Interest-led writing prompts
- Lists of all kinds
- Pen pal letters
- Short stories
- Ideas
- Goals/dreams
- Typing

I love to use Microsoft Word for my kids to do their projects. It is a self-correcting way to work on spelling and grammar. Another favorite is attaching Grammarly to your devices to help perfect writing skills.

There are endless opportunities for kids to dive into writing. Parents have to be able to see them and take advantage of the moments that present themselves.

4-Letter Word

Many people find it easy to see how reading and writing can be learned organically. Math, however, is an entirely different story. We have been programmed to think that math is something we have to cram down a child's throat.

Now, before you put this book down and call me a heretic, listen further. I am not talking about advanced calculus concepts. That can be sought out and learned based on a child's interest and future career path. I am talking about basic arithmetic and even the basics of algebra and geometry. All of these things can be learned in the context of life. Many people struggle with math because it is taught outside of any familiar context. We fail to see how math is all around us.

Did you know that Pythagoras was a musician? Really! He is known for many other things, but this fact astounded me. How we understand music today can be attributed to his application of math to stringed instruments called Pythagorean Tuning. Everything we do involves math in some way, even music.

In the book *Free At Last*, Dan Greenberg talks about an experience he had with math. He set out to prove that the way we were approaching math was all wrong. He attempted to teach a group of kids, ages 9-12, an entire K-6 math textbook from 1898 in 20 contact hours.

This was his observation: *"In 20 contact hours, every single one of the kids knew the material cold. No slackers. No failures. No one "left behind." No "math anxiety." No boredom, frustration, embarrassment. No shame or humiliation. No competition, achievement, failure or success. No prizes. Just 'rithmetic."*

His conclusion, *"Six years of arithmetic can be learned in 20 contact hours if someone is interested."* When someone is interested, something can be learned in a fraction of the time it takes to force them to learn it otherwise.

Beginning your child's journey with numbers as it relates to things we do every single day is the best gift you can give them in developing a strong math sense.

Try exploring how math relates to these areas with your kids. This can be done with all ages.

- Music
- Art
- Maps
- Travel
- Nature
- Gardening/farming
- Food/cooking
- Sports (stats, scores, etc.)
- Board games/card games
- Video games
- Sciences
- Architecture
- Computers/technology
- Dance
- Weather
- Shopping
- Sewing projects
- Money/banking/saving
- Making money
- Measuring sticks (ruler, yard, etc.)
- Gas prices/mileage
- Weights/scales
- Tipping at a restaurant
- Sales tax
- Building projects
- Time

We are gameschoolers! We use games to learn all kinds of things like science, geography, history, and most especially math. Here are our favorite math games.

- Prime Climb
- Mathable
- Cash Flow for Kids
- Ticket to Ride
- Scrabble
- Yahtzee
- Dice Games
- UNO
- Chess
- Monopoly
- Mancala
- Sudoku
- Card games
- Family restaurant
- Family store

As my kids get older and they have clearly marked a path for their future, we begin to formalize math according to their individual goals. Even then, we use life application methods to do so. We utilize math project books, consumer math workbooks, and other resources that help them gain crucial life application skills for their future endeavors.

Chapter 20
What about College?

"The object of education is to prepare the young to educate themselves throughout their lives."

— Robert M Hutchins

Learning comes in many forms. It happens in many ways and at different intervals throughout a person's lifetime. My children have two very different examples of what hard work and determination will get you.

Their dad is a Marine, which is a challenging status to obtain. He later went on to graduate from university and enjoyed a career in retirement education, ministry, management, and banking. When we were in the process of adopting our oldest two children, he went back to school to obtain his MBA. This led to a career in executive leadership as a COO (Chief Operations Officer/Vice President of Operations) in the non-profit sector. He is now an entrepreneur in executive leadership consulting. He worked very hard for his education and is continuing to reap the rewards from what it has afforded him. How did he get there? Hard work, determination, and passion!

I, on the other hand, am a college dropout! Yep! I hated college with a passion. I spent two years at a massive state university and wanted out. I wanted to get on with life now, and ministry was more important to me than anything else. I worked hard at serving and giving of myself. I became an ordained minister in 2001.

Simultaneously, I worked my way up in banking from an entry-level teller to branch management and business lending.

My experiences in management led me to pursue a career in Human Resources. After being an executive recruiter and HR professional for a few years, I became an HR Employee Relations Manager for seven defense manufacturing plants.

I decided to stay at home with our children in 2007. Shortly thereafter, it was impressed upon me to start an advocacy organization for children that has impacted over ten countries around the globe. I train and inspire foster/adoptive parents, social workers, advocates, and government employees that care for vulnerable kids. I have enjoyed and succeeded in three different industries. How on earth did I get here? Hard work, determination, and passion!

Two completely different paths. One included college and one did not. Both of us have had a measure of success we are very proud of and would not change the road that we chose.

Our education system sells the dream to our youth that college is the only way to financial success and happiness. It is setting them up for false expectations and disappointment, not because college is terrible, but because we tell them that the degree is all they need to succeed. They require hard work, determination, and passion! They must have a vision and a mission to make a difference and stand out for their natural gifting. They need soft skills and leadership capabilities. Drive and interpersonal skills are key. These are the things that will get them farther than their peers over anything else.

I support the idea of college. Out of my six children, several may attend. I believe it is a tool for those pursuing a career and vision that require it.

It is foolish to make every child feel like it is a requirement and to treat them as if it is the only way to accomplish their dreams. Many people would argue that college is not just about the education piece. I would say that all of the other benefits of college can be obtained in multiple life scenarios, if they are sought out.

Our goal is to give our children a 360-degree view of every possible option that will get them where they want to go. It is our job to guide and present the best scenarios for their path. That guidance will take into account that child's gifts, temperament, personality, and goals. We give them the option and all the information to make a choice as to which path they want to pursue. College is only one of those options, and it is something they can do after high school or later in life. We cannot reject other options of learning and gaining valuable skills just because they do not fit into a conventional box.

I won't just give you examples like Bill Gates and Steve Jobs and other billionaires who have dropped out of college. They are anomalies, and that is not a fair comparison. Instead, consider the regular people across the world who have attained a measure of success and happiness in their lives. They did it by pursuing something that they love and do really well, instead of following the commonly suggested formula for success. A great book that discusses this further is *Hacking Your Education* by Dale Stephens, founder of Uncollege.

"Our goal is to give our children a 360-degree view of every possible option that will get them where they want to go."

Our goal for our children is that they live out their faith with boldness. We desire that they are happy, healthy, and spend their lives doing something that they love. The road that gets each of them there may be vastly different, and that is okay. College, trade school, workforce, travel, gap year, entrepreneurship – they are all options.

When our children leave our nest, they will be equipped with the spiritual wisdom, soft skills, and hard skills they need to follow their dreams.

Chapter 21
A Day in Our Life

"Learning is not the product of teaching. Learning is the product of the activity of learners."
— John Holt

Most unschooling families would not be able to give you an accurate "Day in the Life" scenario because our days are as unique as the people that are in them. My kids' interests take them in many different directions every day. There is no typical day.

Schedules
I remember way back when we started homeschooling how discouraged I became when I tried to create and follow an overwhelmingly rigid schedule. Time and time again, I felt defeated and incapable of being a good homeschool mom. The problem was I was judging myself by the wrong standards of measurement. I let what everyone else was doing dictate how I felt about what we were doing. It was torture and self-sabotage.

Routines
These days, we do not create or adhere to a schedule unless we have events or appointments that require specific timing. Instead, we flow loosely with a routine. Unschooling is not void of structure. It is just a different kind. My children have extra-curricular activities, sports, and classes they take

outside the home. Time management is a natural learning process.

I love that our routine is relaxed and usually quite predictable, but not unbreakable. Our days generally start in the same way before my kids break off into their own directions.

Facilitator
I consider myself more of a facilitator than a teacher, providing the environment and atmosphere where learning can be inspired. I provide resources to enhance knowledge. My presence to ask the right questions and challenge them to dig for answers is crucial. Instead of telling them what to think, I show them how to think and how to forge a path that is all their own.

I have six uniquely talented and passionate children. I treat them like six entrepreneurs going in different directions. God created them to do something specific. I want to point them in that direction with tools and wisdom for the journey.

"Unschooling is not void of structure. It is just a different kind."

Theme Days
I want to arm my children with all the tools they need to pursue their interests. One way that I do this is through theme day activities. They are very short (one hour) and

always hands-on. Theme days help them practice skills that they can use as they pursue their interests. For the theme day, I will either initiate something fun based on the things they enjoy, or I let them choose what they would like to do. Theme days can take on whatever form, order, or topic that works for you.

The short period of time that we do theme activities is not the only time that they encounter the topics. It is a time to perfect them and have fun doing it. We recognize that they are learning all day, every day.

My teens may or may not take part in our theme days based on other projects they are engaged in. Because they are very focused on their own interests, it is not a priority for them. The only day that is consistent with the older kids is Math Challenge Monday. Their dad will work with them on Consumer Math and Algebra as complements to their respective areas of interest and career paths.

Math Challenge Monday (1 hour)
They can choose a game, activity, project, recipe, or computer resource that exercises numeric skills.

What in the World Tuesday (1 hour)
They choose a book, game, activity, project, or resource that focuses on a person, location in the world, or historical event.

Read about it Wednesday (1 hour)
They (all six kids) choose a book to read to me. This gives me the ability to see how their reading is progressing and help them wherever they need help. This is a time where I get to spend one-on-one time with each kid. While they are

doing art projects or quiet activities, I may put in an audio book.

Write about it Thursday (1 hour)
They choose what they want to write about. It is that simple. I am able to see their progress in grammar, spelling, and other areas by seeing what they choose to write. This allows me to help them in areas they may need it.

Create and Explore Friday (1 hour)
They choose art and/or science projects to explore in any way they desire.

We don't do them every week… maybe one week out of the month. It is important that you not become a slave to theme days. They should not take away from the freedom to explore and follow rabbit trails. The minute you feel overwhelmed or controlled by them, change it up or stop it altogether. This defeats the whole purpose of unschooling.

You may say that sounds like a lot of work. It is! Learning is not linear. It was much easier to sit them all down with a one-size-fits-all boxed curriculum every day and have them answer questions that were not their own. I am willing to inconvenience myself if it means they experience the freedom that comes from unschooling and following their interests.

My days are packed and everyone wants me to get involved in their projects and pursuits. I have to juggle their interests as well as my own. But it is worth it. It leads to a "good kind of tired." I fall in the bed at the end of the day exhausted, but pleased at how much my children have accomplished.

After our brief themed projects or activities, they are free to organize the rest of their day based on what they want to delve into. I just remain available for suggestions, resources, and help. If they are doing a project that requires them to exercise a skill they have never learned, I take the opportunity to teach it to them on the spot. It helps them see how it relates to their interest and life.

Unschooling multiple children

Each child is on a separate path every day, and they may all need you at once. It is much different than sitting down and teaching everyone the same thing. You are literally pulled in all directions. I let them know that I will make it their way and help them in whatever way I can.

I will not pretend that unschooling six children is an easy task. I do try to make sure that I am giving each child and their interests the attention they deserve. Sometimes one child's project takes up an entire day. There could be a season where one child needs me more. This is the case with my daughter who is an author. When it is time to do final edits and publishing, it can take up a large part of my week.

Another example is when my younger children come up with an idea to build or engineer something that needs my oversight or knowledge. It can be a time-consuming endeavor.

Yes! It is a lot of work. However, I would not have it any other way. They have come so far in their maturity and independence in learning that I would not go back to the way we used to do things if you paid me.

DITL

This is a very loose routine. It is the order in which we generally do things, but the actual times could vary significantly. Having a loose routine helps a few of my kids who need to know what comes next.

Morning 7:00-9:00ish
The children wake up when their body has had the proper amount of rest.

9:00-10:30ish
Showers for Mom and six kids

10:30ish
Kids make themselves breakfast

11:00ish
Help out around the house

Noon-ish
Theme Day activity, field trip, or audio/read aloud

1:00-6:00ish
Interest-led pursuits. Lunch when they are hungry.

6:00ish
Dinner

6:30ish
Classes and extra-curricular activities away from home or interest-led pursuits

9:00ish winter/10:00ish summer
Quiet Reading Time with music (no tech)

10:30ish/11:00 p.m.
Most kids are sleeping by this time

11:00-1:00 a.m.
Mom's quiet time and working hours

Because we are year-round learners, we don't separate learning from living. Our weekends look pretty much the same unless we have an event, field trip, family gathering, class, or church to attend. Our days are wide open, free-flowing, and we (parents) stay prepared to delve into whatever our kids find themselves investigating and exploring seven days a week, 365 days a year.

YouTube Companion Video

Channel: Karla and the Sensational Six

Videos:

DITL - A Day in the Life of our Child-Led Learning Family

DITL 2020

Funschooling Theme Days Part 1 - Math Challenge Monday

Funschooling Theme Days Part 2 - What in the World Tuesday

Funschooling Theme Days Part 3 - Read about It Wednesday

Funschooling Theme Days Part 4 - Write about It Thursday

Funschooling Theme Days Part 5 - Create and Explore Fridays

Chapter 22
Keeping Records

"In the end, the secret to learning is so simple: forget about it. Think only of what you love. Follow it, do it, dream about it. One day, you will glance up at your collection of Japanese literature, or trip over the solar oven you built, and it will hit you: learning was there all the time, happening by itself."

— Grace Llewellyn

Let me start by saying that most unschooling families do not go to the extent that I do when it comes to record keeping. I like to have a consistent picture of my children's learning. I live in a state that does not require reporting or testing. However, being an unschooler, I like to be able to present evidence of our learning if/when it is ever requested.

Annual Planning

Every year we sit down with our children and ask them what goals they would like to make for themselves. We look at what they have accomplished in the previous year. They decide if they want to continue exploring current interests and they let us know what new interests they want to jump into.

Going to a new level in reading and writing is always on the list and is still done; however, they choose with the availability of next level resources and ideas.

Living math skills are included on each child's annual goal list and are obtained in hands-on ways until high school age. At that stage, if they have identified which direction they want to pursue, we make sure they have a wide range of resources to choose from to prepare them for that path.

Our annual plans for our teens may look different compared to our younger children. For the younger children, the goals help them gain skills and they do things they enjoy. For our older kids, their plan includes the things that will help them with their future goals for themselves on a more specific level.

Annual plans are always based on our children's interests and not on a scope and sequence based on age, grade, or system. Throughout the year, they add to their goals or change them however they wish based on their interests.

For older children, we investigate what kinds of classes, labs, and experience are needed for the path they want to take and we make sure those things are included in their annual plan.

Everything is a learning experience – EVERYTHING! We honestly believe that life is learning. There is nothing that my children choose to do throughout their day that is fruitless. As a result of that, we have developed an eye for identifying the value in their daily choices and how applicable they are to learning what others consider "schooly" topics.

At the beginning of our transition to this way of living, I kept a journal of everything that my children did each day. I also took lots of pictures of all of their activities and projects. This works for a person who is not going to keep up with an electronic program for record keeping. Eventually, it became frustrating for me because all of my "records" were in different places.

Then I heard about Evernote. I was introduced to it by Sue Elvis, who is an unschooling vlogger/blogger from Australia. This was a significant game changer for me. I was finally able to marry my daily journal with the pictorial evidence of their learning. In 2015, I began keeping all of our daily learning activities in Evernote. This can also be done using OneNote (Microsoft Suite) or other office management software.

Why don't we give grades and scores?
We encourage our children to do their best at the things they choose to master. Being better than you were yesterday is the goal. We don't feel the need to pin a grade or score on what they do. If they have a challenge in an area, we help them overcome it and let them experience the victory of mastering something difficult.

Some may feel that kids need to experience grades or scores to know what college or taking a test is like. They take enough online classes and other activities to understand that without being exposed to the constant stress of grades. If you asked, I could tell you where each of my kids stands in every traditional subject. I want them to enjoy learning and to work hard at goals they set for themselves without the concern of grades.

"We have developed an eye for identifying the value in their daily choices and how applicable they are to learning what others consider "schooly" topics."

How do I keep records without being rigid and methodical?

- I create a notebook in Evernote for each month.
- I create a collection of tags for each child that represents their interests and traditional topics.
- As my children go throughout their day, I snap pictures of their activities and the process of their projects and experiments.
- I post those projects into Evernote with an explanation, pictures, and links about the activity.
- I then tag the post by child and topic.
- I can go back at any time and add to these posts.

At the end of a year, I can pull up a child's tag on a particular topic and see how many times they had learning opportunities in a specific area. For example, I can pull up my oldest son and see how many times in 2017 he did a project, watched a show, or read a book about physics. Or I can pull up another child and see how many times they did a project or activity that involved math skills. All the posts for that year and that topic will come up, and I can see their continual progress in an area that is completely interest-led.

We know learning is always taking place. It is impossible for me to capture every single thing that they are learning. I do my best to represent the majority of their activities, but I do not fret or get bent out of shape if I miss something. The kids get my attention if they have a project or activity they are working on so I can observe it and snap a picture.

How do I keep records and transcripts for older kids? This process is very similar to how I do it for my younger children. The purpose is more specific to their plans.

- I create a notebook under each child's name.
- Within the notebook, I create folders/notes with the titles of all the things that interest them and the things they spend the most time exploring.
- Their notebooks also keep in mind the requirement of the trade school, college, or job that each kid is pursuing.
- Every time they complete an online class, read a book, go on a field trip, do a lab, project, or activity, I put the information under that topic/course, along with all the pictures, links, and resources used.

- I track how often they engage with these topics via their topic tags.

- These records are ready-made transcripts and pictorial yearbooks when the time comes for them to apply for a scholarship, job, college, or trade school. It also helps them create an impressive resume.

Many unschooling families don't go through the trouble of doing much of what I have shared here. I do it because I am a visual person and I want my children's learning to be represented in an organized fashion even though they are unschoolers.

YouTube Companion Videos

Channel: Karla and the Sensational Six

Videos:
Part 1 - Annual Planning for Interest-Led Learners
Part 2 - Annual Planning for Interest-Led Learners
Part 1 - Interest-Led Learning with Evernote
Part 2 - Interest-Led Learning with Evernote

SAMPLE DOCUMENT
Annual Goal Form

Name:

Calendar Year:

Current Passions/Interests/Projects:
(example: What are they currently pursuing, interested in, or working on?)

New interests/topics:
(example: Have they mentioned new ideas, interests, or classes that they want to take?)

Important Life Skills:
(example: Living Math, Reading, Writing)

Life Skill Integration:
(How will reading and writing be integrated into their interests and daily life? How will we expose living math in everyday life?)

Teen Planning:
(What exposure will prepare them for their individual path?)

360-Degree View Options:
(What are all of the possible ways to achieve their career goals – working, college, travel, business, etc.?)

Classes/Books/Field Trips/Website Ideas:
(example: Collect resources here)

Annual Goals:
(These goals are made up of the info you collected from the above sections)

Chapter 23
Every Day is NOT Rosy

"Strong-willed children become adults who change the world as long as we can hang on for the ride and resist the temptation to 'tame' the spirit out of them."
— Sarah Stogryn

We have our challenges. I don't want to make it seem like every day is rosy. I am a mother of six very vocal, strong-willed, and passionate children. They have squabbles, opinions, likes, dislikes, feelings, and hormones. There is no way that you can live in a household with eight completely separate human beings and have every day go flawlessly.

There are days we spend more time on character and attitude adjustments than on creating or learning something amazing. We overcome our challenges with prayer and talking things out.

Seasons

Each of my children goes through seasons where they suck up every bit of knowledge they can on a topic. Then there are other seasons when they want to chill and learn different things. I have noticed that deep and meaningful learning comes in spurts. Unschooling allows that to happen without the fear that the kids are "behind." From the surface, it may look like there is no learning going on. It is not true. Learning comes in waves.

Regular Days

Most days are not full of fireworks and brilliant discoveries of epic proportions. They are regular days. You have to be comfortable with those days and not put undue pressure on yourself or your kids to produce or manufacture forced results.

Boredom

Boredom is good. I love it when my children get bored. I genuinely believe it is the breeding ground for creativity. The ideas, learning, and exploration that take place when kids get bored are priceless. I have a "Mom, I am Bored" list hanging on our homeschool closet. It lists several things my kids can do when they are bored or restless.

Speaking of boredom, there is a day that I will not forget. I had just organized my closets and created my awesome carts. I came home later that day to see things thrown all over the place and projects in multiple stages. I was furious. How could they destroy my beautifully organized, perfectly categorized systems? What I wanted was happening, and all I could think about was how their creativity ruined my order. They stood there confused by my irritation. When I stepped back and paid attention, they were solving their boredom with creativity – this is precisely what I wanted them to do. That day Mommy got a checkup from the neck up.

Play

Take play seriously. Many times we separate play and learning as if they are opposites. Play is learning. Children, and dare I say adults as well, learn most when they are relaxed and exploring a topic of interest. Do not underestimate play.

"I love it when my children get bored. I truly believe it is the breeding ground for creativity."

Hard Things

How do kids learn to do hard things? Won't children think that everything is fun and that they will always get their way if you raise them like this?

When given the freedom to pursue something that they are passionate about, they will run into bumps in the road. It is at that point that they dig in and do what is necessary to accomplish that goal. A passionate person is a person with vision. If they see the end goal, they will remain encouraged along the way. The "hard stuff" in the middle is just a step in that direction.

As I was writing this book, I decided to ask a couple of my children about doing hard things. Why do you choose to do something that is challenging?

Daughter (15)
"I love to write the first draft of my books. I detest the process of rewriting, changing, and editing them. I do it because I want a good product and the reward at the end is an excellent book!"

Son (14)
"I like the challenge of math, but I don't like it when it gets hard. I keep going because I know it will be useful for me in my future career."

Both kids expressed the discomfort of hard things, but they acknowledged the reward of doing it anyway. When you have a vision and you want it badly enough, you will do the hard things without force.

Chapter 24
Gifted and Special Needs Unschooling

"Every child is an artist. The problem is how to remain an artist once he grows up."
— Pablo Picasso

Unschooling is indeed a blessing for those who are gifted. I, myself, have several children who are intellectually gifted, one of which can take in information faster than the speed of light. This child has to be free and allowed to move leaps and bounds forward in short periods of time. Any "teaching" or "structured learning" I have attempted in the past has led to frustration. The thirst for more outgrows my capacity to supply it when I depend on my knowledge and experience alone.

Unschooling has allowed my children to create expertise for themselves that they never would have had the time or freedom to pursue if we tried things traditionally. Letting them fly solo has turned out to be a beautiful self-discovery of their depth and extensive knowledge. There is no end to the levels they can reach or the expertise they can obtain when learning has no barriers, framework, or limits.

I also have a few children who would be considered 2e (twice exceptional). It means that they boast both giftedness and at least one learning challenge simultaneously. Engaging their interests has closed the gap between that giftedness and learning challenge. I have found that their challenges cause them to aggressively seek and create bridges to compensate for and neutralize their struggles. With our support, they learn to do this on their own.

Special Needs Unschooling

My Sensational Six represent a wide range of giftedness and special needs. Among my crew, we have reading challenges (Dyslexia), math challenges (Dyscalculia), writing challenges (Dysgraphia), and attention deficits. We don't allow labels to define our children. What I love about this learning environment is that it squashes all perceptions of what a person can or cannot do.

One of my children has a challenge with calculation and math concepts. It has always been a struggle. Her gifting is so strong in other areas that we would be negligent to ignore her natural talents. We expose her to the basics for the direction that she desires to go. However, we focus more on her strengths, dreams, and potential. We do this with all of our kids. Unschooling allows us to do that.

Another child struggles with the ability to write fluently. The connection between his brilliant thoughts and the page is a painful (physically and mentally) process. He has no shortage of stories or information to share. We make sure that he has other tools to express his brilliance to the world like typing, voice-to-text software, and dictation. It restores confidence in a learning atmosphere that does not see challenges as a roadblock.

Trauma and Learning

I have found that unschooling is particularly effective with children who have suffered traumatic events in their lives.

Trauma can affect a child's ability to learn and grow in a traditional learning environment. In the line of work that I am in, I have seen many children misdiagnosed with ADHD, when in fact they had PTSD as a result of early childhood trauma. This affects all aspects of their lives.

For example, a child who struggles with ADHD or emotional regulation can perfect a skill and interest with pride while having the room to work on their challenges. Approaching it this way brings confidence and the ability to be highlighted for their strengths instead of weaknesses.

"What I love about this learning environment is that it squashes all perceptions of what a person can or cannot do."

Chapter 25
Interest-Led Summers/Weekends

"Learning is not a product of teaching. Kids are born learning. They learn how to walk, how to talk. They're basically little scientists. If we don't stop that process, it will continue."
— Grace Llewellyn

You may have read this entire book and loved everything about it, yet none of it fits your situation. Maybe your children are in public or private school, so you have little control over their learning environment. Homeschooling may not be possible for you at the moment. You may even be a homeschool mom who is not ready to dive into unschooling or have a spouse who is not supportive of this change. It is still possible to create an atmosphere in your home that encourages your children's interests. You still have the ability to turn your home into a hub of creativity and inspiration. Here are some keys to help you get started.

- Avoid over-scheduling your child's summer, evenings, and weekends with random camps and activities to keep them busy.

- Allow your kids to have downtime. Let them get bored. What they choose to do will give you clues.

- If you do sign them up for anything, let it be an activity or camp that reflects their interests.

- Spend time discussing their interests and goals for themselves.

- Tour industry-specific companies, related museums, and other places that will give them more information and inspiration toward their interests.

- Frequent the library to encourage them to read about their interests while they have extra time outside of the school year schedule.

- Provide an environment and a creative space for exploration at home of new and exciting things both about their current interests and new ideas.

- Figure out how to rearrange their school year activities to include their interests all year long.

- Take time to engage your children in what they are learning at school. Talk about it and try to help them relate it to life. Encourage them to dig deeper into the things that interest them at school and elsewhere. Present reading and learning as something that is enjoyable instead of something dreadful to avoid.

- It will be essential to put just as much, or more, effort and joy into their interests as you put on grades, tests, and academic accomplishments. It will give them encouragement to pursue things they love and stick with it!

Part Four: What's Next?

Chapter 26
Follow Your OWN Dreams

"Anyone who stops learning is old, whether this happens at twenty or eighty. Anyone who keeps on learning not only remains young but becomes constantly more valuable regardless of physical capability."
— Harvey Ullman

You have heard all this talk about dreams, passions, goals, and the interests of your children. What about you? What are your interests and aspirations? What passions have you laid down in the name of motherhood martyrdom?

Your kids spend more time watching you than listening to you. What are they seeing? As parents, we owe it to our children to go for big things with the same gusto that we use to encourage them.

I can hear all the excuses because I have made them myself. When the kids are adults, I will write my book. When I have more money, I will start my business. When I lose weight, I will have more confidence to get my dream job. Our lists can go on and on until we give up on our passion altogether.

God created YOU to do something that no other person on the face of this earth can do. We tend to believe that about our children but forget about God's divine purpose for us, outside of motherhood. You are not doing yourself or your children any favors by pretending that being a mom is your only purpose in life. Somebody somewhere is depending on you to do what God has called you to do.

As I said in a previous chapter, I believe we can have it all, just not all at the same time or in the same season. Know what season you are in and begin to walk toward your passion with joy.

I have been there. I have struggled with my role as a mom and the passions that stir within me. In an unschooling household, my husband and I have found ourselves unschooling as well. It just becomes part of the atmosphere. When we are fulfilled, we are happier people. I am a happier mom because I realized God's call on my own life. I can share that with my children. As long as my marriage and home are my priority, pursuing my passion is a God thing!

After adopting our first three children, I became a very vocal advocate for kids in foster care and around the world. My advocacy led to a radio program with a global following that focused on foster care, adoption, and international missions.

After a year of hosting the Family by Design radio program, I began to get invitations to speak throughout the U.S. My passion is to see kids loved, nurtured, and cared for in a family setting, and to help parents understand the vast effects of trauma on the kids in their care. My career was taking on a form I never planned. With the support of my husband and children along the way, I began to accept this new road I was on.

In 2014, I was asked to accompany a group to Ethiopia and Ghana to conduct training for social workers in both countries. It was a game changer and began a snowball effect that only God could have planned. Since 2014, I have conducted consultations, training, and conferences throughout the U.S., Ethiopia, Ghana, South Africa, Zimbabwe, Malawi, Thailand, Costa Rica, and twice in Mexico.

"You are not doing yourself or your children any favors by pretending that being a mom is your only purpose in life."

It has been a whirlwind of surprises and such a blessing to be able to do what I do. I cannot pretend that it has always been easy. With the help of my husband, I have been able to keep my household and family at the forefront of my focus. 85% of my time is committed to my family and 15% of my time is spent traveling and writing materials for my organization called iSpeak4KidsGlobal. I also have several books that I am writing, which has always been a dream of mine.

I do conferences within my state and throughout the U. S. a couple of times a year. I also accept one to two international invitations a year that can be seven- to fourteen-day trips. We are thankful that my husband can handle everything on the home front during my travels. The rest of my time is dedicated to being a wife and mother. I love that!

It is such a privilege to be able to do both. You can too. There is something God put on the inside of you that is roaring to get out. Your children need to see you reach and work toward your passions. They will learn to do it themselves by watching your example.

- Let them inspire you
- Let them see your faith
- Let them see you struggle

- Let them see you sweat
- Let them see you invest
- Let them see you juggle fire
- Let them see you give to others
- Let them see you fail and not give up
- Let them see you break barriers
- Let them feel your encouragement
- Let them pursue their dreams NOW

When your children see you do these things, they will look at the possibilities for themselves against all the odds. I genuinely believe that I had the confidence to help my children pursue their interests and passions because I did it myself. Don't just encourage your kids to go for the gold. Go for it yourself, whatever that may look like for you. God already knows.

What dream(s) have you let fade?

What excuse(s) have you used to keep you from pursuing them?

What can you do today to begin a journey towards them?

How can you share those endeavors with your children?

Chapter 27
Where do YOU go from Here?

"I've concluded that genius is as common as dirt. We suppress our genius only because we haven't yet figured out how to manage a population of educated men and women. The solution, I think, is simple and glorious. Let them manage themselves."
— John Taylor Gatto

You chose to read this book for a reason. Only you know what that reason is. My prayer is that you have been able to see the value in following your child's lead in their learning. You may choose unschooling or only aspects of it to give your kids more autonomy in their education. Either will be a valuable experience for your homeschool.

What parts of this book do you identify with the most?

What parts of unschooling are attractive to you? Why?

List new ideas that you want to try in your homeschool.

In what areas can you loosen up and give your kids more autonomy?

In what ways can your children practice and live out their dreams now?

Epilogue

"I never teach my pupils; I only provide the conditions in which they can learn."
— Albert Einstein

If you are looking for a long list of "unschooling rules," you will not find them. Unschooling is different for every family and every child. It is the freedom to follow and explore your interests.

Unschooling is not a promise that your child will be the next Einstein or Nobel Prize winner. It does not mean that their success will be exponentially more significant than everyone else's. There are no guarantees with public school, private school, traditional homeschooling, or even college. Likewise, unschooling does not guarantee financial success or happiness.

What unschooling or interest-led learning, when done well, can ensure is that your child's dreams and their interests are valued. They have a chance to pursue them and explore the world around them as they grow into adulthood. How much further would many of us be if we were given the chance as children to follow our interests and have a head start towards our life's passion(s)?

I do not claim to be an expert on preparing YOUR child for their future. I can only share and encourage families based on what has worked well for us and the joy that we have experienced by taking this leap.

We are not raising our children to fit into someone else's mold or plan. It is not our goal to compete for academic prowess or an Ivy League scholarship. We do not strive to force or coerce our children to live up to a standard that does not define who they are as individuals. We encourage them to be their best selves according to God's plan for them. As parents, we are confident that God has equipped us to guide them and encourage them as they move toward the next stages of their lives.

Again, learning is a lifelong journey! It is not to be boxed or limited to specific days of the week, hours of the day, or times of the year. If we are breathing, we are learning. Our children's brains don't turn on at 8 a.m. and shut off at 3 p.m. Neither should their learning environment be limited by these standards of measurement.

I pray that the experiences, examples, and wisdom that we have gained throughout our transition to unschooling have been a blessing to you and your family.

Stay tuned for the follow-up to this book: *Homeschool Gone Wild ~ Interest-Led Learning into Adulthood*, that will focus on our high school journey and transition as our children enter adulthood, college, and the workforce.

Karla Marie Williams

Definitions

Radical Unschooling - Living as if school does not exist. Parenting your children as a partner and respectfully allowing autonomy in all areas.

Unschooling - Living as if school does not exist. Learning through life and experiences versus formalized lessons. May or may not subscribe to all radical unschooling principles.

Interest-Led Learning - Similar to unschooling but tunnel focused on a direction chosen by the child and facilitated and encouraged by the parent. The way that this process looks can look "schooly" for some children and more "unschooly" for others depending on the child's chosen field of study or career.

Worldschooling - Literally learning from the world around you. Mainly refers to families that travel often and use cultural experiences and awareness as a primary way of learning.

Strewing - Unforced placement of resources that will enhance the passion and interest of a child without expectation or requirement.

P.U.P. - Periodic Unschoolers Panic

Notes

Chapter 4
John Holt, author, and father of unschooling/self-directed education

How Children Learn, by John Holt

Chapter 5
Five Love Languages of Children by Gary Chapman 1997

Chapter 7
Survey of Grown Unschoolers by Peter Gray, Ph.D. Psychology Today 2014

Chapter 8
Compulsory Education, www.findlaw.com

Chapter 14
Unschooling Rules by Clark Aldrich Page 61 Expose More, Teach Less

Chapter 18
www.unschoolrules.com

Chapter 19
Free At Last by Dan Greenberg 1987

Pythagorean Tuning Wikipedia

Chapter 20
Hacking Your Education by Dale Stephens, founder of Uncollege

Chapter 22
Sue Elvis, Stories of an Unschooling Family, Australia

Connect with Karla

Facebook
Karla and the Sensational Six

BeBold Publishing

Instagram
Karla and the Sensational 6

YouTube
Karla and the Sensational Six

Website
karlamariewilliams.com

Made in the USA
Las Vegas, NV
05 January 2022

40323584R00095